Commitment to SERVICE

THE LIBRARY'S MISSION

Commitment to SERVICE

THE LIBRARY'S MISSION

ALPHONSE F. TREZZA, Editor

A CONFERENCE SPONSORED BY THE FLORIDA STATE UNIVERSITY SCHOOL OF LIBRARY AND INFORMATION STUDIES AND THE CENTER FOR PROFESSIONAL DEVELOPMENT AND PUBLIC SERVICE

G.K. HALL & CO.
BOSTON

Commitment to Service: The Library's Mission

Edited by Alphonse F. Trezza

by G.K. Hall & Co.
70 Lincoln Street
Boston, Massachusetts 02111

The paper used in this publication meets the minimum requirements of American National Standard for Information Sciences – Permanence of Paper for Printed Library Materials, ANSI Z39.48-1984. ∞™

10 9 8 7 6 5 4 3 2 1

Library of Congress Cataloging-in-Publication Data

Commitment to service : the library's mission / Alphonse F. Trezza, editor.
ISBN – 0-8161-1931-7
p. cm. – (Professional librarian series)
"The 1989 Library Conference . . . held March 12-15, 1989 at the Florida State Conference Center . . . jointly sponsored by the Florida State University School of Library and Information Studies and the Center for Professional Development and Public Service" – Pref.
Includes bibliographical references.
1. Libraries – Aims and objectives – Congresses.
2. Library science – Philosophy – Congresses.
3. Libraries and readers – Congresses. I. Trezza, Alphonse F. II. Library Conference (1989 : Florida State University) III. Florida State University. School of Library and Information Studies. IV. Florida State University. Center for Professional Development and Public Service. V. Series.
Z678.C737 1990
025.5 – dc20 89-26905
CIP

MANUFACTURED IN THE UNITED STATES OF AMERICA.

Contents

Preface

The 1989 Florida State University Library Conference, held 12-15 March 1989, at the Florida State Conference Center, addressed the theme "Commitment to Service: The Library's Mission." The conference was sponsored jointly by the Florida State University School of Library and Information Studies and the Center for Professional Development and Public Service.

The papers presented at the conference and gathered here in this volume demonstrate the breadth of knowledge, vitality, and commitment of librarians throughout our country to the ideal of library service. As documented by the papers, these qualities are forged and tempered daily, as obstacles continually arise, and lead to the development of superior and continually changing library services. Marketing, facts and figures, and continual monitoring of and refining of programs in place are emphasized in the committed librarians and libraries portrayed here. The often unstated "I-can-do-everything-super-librarian" assumption has given way to the more profitable "maximize-the-effectiveness-of-resources" and "don't-be-shy-of-stating-needs" modes of thinking necessary to build and maintain successful library programming.

The authors repeatedly refer to their intention to cause discomfort by what they say. It is hoped that the reader will indeed use any occasional discomfort experienced as he or she reads as an opportunity to reassess the cherished belief or set of beliefs under attack at that particular moment.

The keynote address was presented by W. David Penniman, director of library and information systems for AT&T Bell Laboratories, and president of the American Society for Information Science. Entitled "Serving the Public – Philosophy, Attitude, and Commitment," the address sounded the keynote of the conference: service in a market-driven environment.

Penniman came to his position one week after the dramatic AT&T divestiture. Penniman clearly believes that this epoch-making event in the life of one of the biggest corporations in the U.S. can serve as an example to all who work in services of the profound changes under way today in the environment in which we conduct business.

Through examples taken from his accomplishments at AT&T, Penniman built his case for information services and their dollars and cents relevance to society and our economy. Further, he emphasized the importance of framing the message about information services in measurable outputs and dollars and cents inputs. This way, one can make no mistake about its relevance to decisionmakers' needs, and information services can find their place in the realistic priorities of society or the organization.

The second general session was organized around the theme "Reference Services for Today and Tomorrow." The presentations focused on traditional, present high-technology and possible future high-technology reference delivery systems.

"Traditional Reference Services in Today's Library" was the title of the paper given by Andrew M. Hansen, executive director of the reference and adult services division of the American Library Association. Hansen provided a historical overview of the development of today's reference services and analyzed some of the issues that challenge them today, such as "fee or free" and the recommendations forthcoming from the ALA Presidential Committee on Information Literacy, published at the 1989 midwinter ALA meeting.

Michael McGill, vice-president for research at the Online Computer Library Center (OCLC), presented a paper called "Impact of Technology on Today's Reference Services." In it, he outlined what OCLC is doing to enhance reference service. Further, he shared his vision of the future. He summarized some previous computer developments in order to provide a flavor of that sector of technology and asserted that he believes that dependence of academic and other reference departments on computers will continue to increase. The power of the personal computer, networked and backed up with mass storage devices, will continue to revolutionize the lives of "information rich" institutions while making it more difficult for the "information poor" in our society as they attempt to survive. The closing paper in this group, entitled "Changing Technology and Tomorrow's Reference Services," was presented by Thomas J. Galvin, executive director of the American Library Association. Citing at the outset his own poor record for predicting the future, Galvin plunged on to frame the challenge for tomorrow's reference services as that of raising the level of the information literacy of the nation. He emphasized the all-encompassing nature of information literacy as he sees it – that the reference services of tomorrow will concentrate not on document delivery but on information transfer. Creativity will be at the center of this revolution, and virtually every cherished notion about reference services will be brought under scrutiny. He finished by citing innovative academic research libraries that lead the way today in responding to this challenge.

The third general session's theme was "Resource Sharing and Collection Development." This session featured two presentations which outlined the historical background of these two cornerstones of library philosophy and practice.

David H. Brunell, executive director of the Bibliographic Center for Research, Inc., presented his paper entitled "ILL: The Backbone of Materials Sharing." Brunell outlined the early history of interlibrary loan and then painted a detailed and encouraging picture of the growth of ILL as well as the influences, both positive and negative, that he sees as critical to its development. His spotlighting of highly effective programs in Illinois, Pennsylvania, and the western United States, each developed under different assumptions and with different outcomes, provided a glimpse of the diversity and innovativeness of library professionals working on the cutting edge to share resources.

"Collection Development and the Influence of Resource Sharing" provided perspective on the influence of a resource sharing environment on collection development. Anthony W. Ferguson, library resources director at Columbia University Libraries, presented this paper.

Ferguson traced the history of resource sharing in this country, rightly pointing out the intense pride, both individual and institutional, that precluded cooperation among early American academic libraries. Moving to a treatment of the present situation, Ferguson discussed roadblocks to resource sharing, listing them as "lacks, fears, and difficulties." He has seen signs that electronic technology can make up for some of the difficulties, that the fears are starting to be addressed through the Research Libraries Group Cooperative Collecting Responsibility initiative, and that the lack will be made up when and if institutional and individual pride can be overcome to allow resources to be reallocated across institutions. The example of materials related to mathematics held by RLG libraries gave a very instructive look at how this can work best.

Concurrent sessions were held and repeated, on the following themes: services for children and young people, services to adults and to special populations, and serving the university family–students, faculty and staff.

Mary R. Somerville, children's coordinator of the Broward County Public Library, Fort Lauderdale, presented a paper entitled "Slaying Dragons: Overcoming Obstacles to Excellence in Youth Services." For Somerville, the dragons to be overcome are (1) cynicism, (2) the notion that children and young adults will settle for mediocre service because they are somehow "not quite bright" or unsophisticated, and (3) ingrained habit and negative thinking about services in general and children's services in particular. Other issues treated as Somerville disposed of the dragons one by one were the need for better information on which to base requests for budget increases in order to provide adequate funding for programming; the professional image of children's and young adult's librarians; the increased need for youth services in light of present social, demographic, and immigration trends; and the increased recognition starting to be accorded children's librarianship at the national level by the American Library Association and other professional organizations.

A presentation by Judith L. Williams, director of the Jacksonville Public Libraries, looked at adults and a second, by Professor Gerald Jahoda of the School of Library and Information Studies, Florida State University, addressed special populations.

Williams's paper, "Free for All," applied many of the concepts of the Penniman lecture at the level of the public library. She spoke of the pressures of developing a library system in a high-growth area where all the other city services have needs growing as fast as, if not faster than, those of the library. Drawing imagery from American populist and patriotic literature, she touched on many public library issues and gave a vivid portrait of the vital organization she heads. Williams addresses the serious problem of the proliferation of fees and makes a strong case for free service. The question and answer session following her presentation was a gold mine of specific, practical solutions to public library administrative problems.

Jahoda's short paper, "Public Library Service to Special Groups," situated the special patron squarely in the mainstream, citing the statistic that eighty-five million U. S. citizens fall in the category for one reason or another. From there, he outlined the necessary and sufficient conditions for serving the special patron.

Paula Kaufman, dean of libraries at the University of Tennessee, presented a paper about university clients (students, faculty, and staff). Entitled "Serving the University Family: Truths Among the Myths," the paper listed five myths about university library services: (1) University libraries provide services to most of the students, faculty, and staff in their institutions; (2) Good service means more, not less, and good service is cumulative; (3) University librarians know what their users want; (4) Services and OPACs are designed for users; and (5) University libraries operate efficiently and effectively for their users.

Kaufman touched on trends affecting service in the academic library, finishing by emphasizing the need to assess constantly the needs of users and to approach users not only as librarians but as fellow researchers in order to understand more fundamentally the needs of today's researchers and anticipate those needs when reforming and reevaluating services.

John B. Duff, commissioner of the Chicago Public Library, presented the Samuel Lazerow Memorial Lecture, "Breaking Ground in Chicago: Planning the Harold Washington Library Center." The paper provided a succinct introduction to some of the thinking behind general design concepts to be implemented in the new Chicago Public Library building, the construction of which started in 1989.

The papers from the final session of the conference treated different aspects of the session theme: impact of technology on staffing.

Ann E. Prentice is vice president for library and information resources at the University of South Florida. Prentice's presentation was entitled "Implications of Technology on Staffing." It reviewed the needs of both the staff members and the library organization as the process of technological evolution/revolution transforms the library in the near future. She emphasized the degree and speed of change apparent in the last few decades and contrasted it with what had occurred in the previous two hundred to five hundred years since the introduction of printing with movable type. She recommended that librarians take the widest possible view in order to choose actively the future they want for their libraries and librarians.

Elizabeth Smith Aversa's paper, "Information Specialist–A Modern Day Librarian or A New Professional?" discussed the definitions of terms in the fields of library science, information science, and related fields. Aversa is assistant professor, College of Library and Information Services, University of Maryland. This paper provided an excellent overview of terms used in the field and descriptions of those using them. Citing Moore, Slater, and King Research, as well as other occupational literature, Aversa showed the inherent conflict among the different existing definitions in the fields, pointing out strengths and weaknesses of each.

The twelve papers presented at the conference provided a thoughtful review of many issues attendant to the library's services to its public. The challenges are many–the papers serve a useful purpose only if the ideas, suggestions, and comments result in actions, decisions, and improved services. Money isn't the only solution to our problems. Cost-effective management, priority setting, and the ability to make difficult decisions regarding the services to be offered or discontinued are a more positive approach to the problems and challenges we face.

TERENCE F. SEBRIGHT, Director
Technical Services
Mills Memorial Library
Rollins College
Winter Park, Florida

ALPHONSE F. TREZZA, Professor
School of Library and Information Studies
Florida State University
Tallahassee, Florida

Acknowledgments

Appreciations and thanks go to the administration of Florida State University and the School of Library and Information Studies for their support of this annual library conference.

Thanks also go to the staff of the Center for Professional Development and Public Service at Floridat State University for their role in providing the excellent facilities and arrangements so important to the success of their conference and to the State Library of Florida for providing, through LSCA Title I funds, for the distribution of copies of the proceedings to the public libraries in Florida.

Introduction: Serving the Public – Philosophy, Attitude, and Commitment

W. DAVID PENNIMAN
Director
Library and Information Systems
AT&T Bell Labs
Murray Hill, New Jersey

I plan to discuss four areas:

- Libraries and the library profession as viewed by others in the field.
- Which leads to a paradox we all must grapple with.
- How this paradox has influenced my views on technology and management issues we all face as information professionals.
- Finally, what it means to be a leader today and how we must rise to the leadership challenge.

I am certainly not alone in the message I bring to you. I've collected the thoughts of a number of other library leaders on the issues I want to discuss and would like to lay some groundwork with their words. Wilfred Lancaster says of librarians, "The survival of the library profession depends on its ability and willingness to change its emphasis and image."[1] In the *Journal of the American Society for Information Science* (ASIS), an article by two other librarians states, "Library administrators have the responsibility to create organizational climates that encourage and promote change. Traditional committee structures are an insufficient approach to anticipate and meet the challenges. Experimentation is essential, improvisation inevitable, and the sharing of both successes and failures a professional and organizational imperative. The great responsibility, however, rests with the individual who must adapt, and adopt the idea of continual change as a goal and a mode of both personal and organizational operation."[2] Pat Battin says, "One of the most powerful deterrents to change in conservative institutions is the existence of strong autonomous vested interests and the fear of losing one's empire."[3] (I'll argue in this paper that without change, the empire as such will be lost).

Lewis Branscomb agrees. About librarians, he states, "If libraries are to play a creative role in this period of experimentation, they must again become teachers and innovators, and not custodians, lest the treasures in their custody are made obsolete by alternative services that fail to serve humanity as imaginatively and profoundly as they could."[4] Daniel Boorstin has said, "Libraries remain the meccas of self help, the most open of open universities . . . where there are no entrance examinations and no diplomas, and where one can enter at any age."[5] There are other images of libraries. From a novelist who wrote on the romantic possibilities of a public library in Southern California, we hear, "We don't use the Dewey decimal classification or any index system to keep track of our books. We record their entrance into the library contents ledger and then give them back to its author who is free to place it anywhere he wants in the library, on whatever shelf catches his fancy. . . ." (Remind you of some your shelvers?) This author continues, "It doesn't make any difference where a book is placed because nobody ever checks them out and nobody ever comes here to read them. This is not that kind of library. This is another kind of library."[6]

The Paradox of Change

This leads me to the paradox of change. To keep from becoming that other kind of library, to remain Boorstin's mecca of self help, we must be committed to change and be in control of that change. If we do nothing or do as we have done in the past, we will change–but for the worse. Our institutions and systems will degrade. For we are in a changing environment; to survive, we must adapt. To restate the paradox: To remain what we are, we must change; if we do not change, we won't remain what we are.

For the past five years, I have been struggling with this paradox in a company that has been struggling with it also on a ground scale. As with libraries, AT&T had a long-standing commitment to service (in their case, universal telephone service). As many libraries do, AT&T felt it had a right to a protected environment, one in which its future must be assured for the benefit of all. But the environment was changing, and many could have (and did) try to tell this giant that a new day was coming. When it finally did arrive in January 1984, few were prepared for or understood the demands the new environment would place upon them. It was into this setting that I arrived, one week after divestiture occurred. I came preaching change to this premier private industrial library network. I came with many years of experience in information systems, much of it as a change agent, but I was still unprepared for the deeply imbedded culture and context of an organization noted for excellence that was achieved in a setting that no longer existed.

So the challenge was and still is: how to maintain excellence in a changing environment where responsiveness to customers determines who will survive. That is your environment, too. You all have customers and sooner or later their satisfaction with your services and their willingness to continue to support you will determine your survival. Coming to grips with this inevitable truth–your survival depends on satisfying your customers–is surprisingly difficult for many organizations that are, in fact, in the service business. Recognizing that those who make funding decisions are one type of customer, while those who receive your service are another type, is important in establishing your customer performance measures and strategies. I'll speak more about performance measures later. There are a variety of ways to fail but only one way to succeed–continuous monitoring and improvement across all your customer segments.

Facts and History of the Information Vending Industry

I'll discuss briefly some key areas that can help us in the quest for customer satisfaction and survival. First, how big an issue are we dealing with? Let me give you some data from a monetary viewpoint: The information vending industry (actually a series of information industries) has revenues exceeding $16 billion annually. Volume is expected to grow to $50 billion in the 1990s. Yet this is only the tip of the iceberg. Users of internally generated information account for ten times that volume of purchased information in business throughout the U.S.[7] In the publishing arena, over $5 billion are spent in the general interest area alone.[8] In the library arena, including federal, public, academic and school libraries, budgets match or equal revenues of the general publishing industry, in excess of $6 billion per year.[9] These dollar-oriented numbers argue for careful attention in any economic environment, but in an increasingly competitive setting they demand that we keep our eye on customer satisfaction, or someone else will, even in the public sector.

Other numbers would seem to point toward technology as an environmental factor to pay attention to. I'll look briefly at four information-related measures that can help us focus our energies and resources where they count. For at least two of the following four measures, I am indebted to Hal Becker, who published a delightful article concerning the expanded rate at which data have been stored and transmitted.[10] The measures I'm going to describe relate significantly to our concern with the future of libraries.

In 490 B.C. the fastest way to send a message was by human messenger, running as fast as he could for as far as he could. Often he dropped dead upon completing the task (or was killed if the content of the message was displeasing). The data rate for that "system" was well under one word per minute (probably closer to one hundredth of a word per minute, depending upon message length). Despite experiments with semaphore towers, carrier pigeons, and horseback riders, no universal breakthrough came until the 1840s. That was the year of the invention of telegraphy. With this technology, transmission rates achieved a level of about fifty words per minute. Now we have reached rates of one billion words per minute, and by the 1990s the figure will exceed 100 trillion words per minute.

Storage capacity has made similar startling advances. In 4000 B.C. characters were stored on clay tablets at about one per cubic inch. Papyrus scrolls later improved the situation somewhat. It wasn't until A.D. 1450, however, with the advent of the printing press using movable type, that mass storage became widely available in books holding up to five hundred characters per cubic inch. With high-density electronic, magnetic, or optical technology, this figure has been pushed to astounding levels. By A.D. 2000 the capability to store 125 billion characters per cubic inch will be realized.

Two other significant areas exist. Each has been a major barrier to effective information handling. One has only recently been resolved; the other remains a challenge.

Computation rates have been measured in instructions per second for some time. For most of that time, beginning in 5000 or 500 B.C. (authorities differ on its age), a single device held the world's speed record for computation when in the hands of an expert. That device was the abacus, and the rate was literally a handful of computations or instructions per second (probably two to four). It wasn't until the mid-1940s, with the development of the electronic computer, that this figure jumped significantly. Then the rate of growth became phenomenal. In a few decades the figure rose from hundreds to hundreds of thousands to one million, then to ten to fifty million. A rate well beyond one hundred million instructions per second (perhaps exceeding a billion) is not unexpected with new computer architecture.

The second factor is that of our own symbol-processing capability. Around 4000 to 3500 B.C., when the first written language emerged, humans were capable of processing about three hundred words or symbols per minute. Even with speed reading and listening devices and various other techniques, there have been no order-of-magnitude changes in this figure like those we have seen in the measures for transmission, storage, and processing. This last barrier is symbolic, I believe, of an even greater barrier – our limited ability to make sense out of all this information being stored, processed, and transmitted.

Understanding the New Technology: A Model for Change

In a recently published book entitled *Information Anxiety*, the author defines the meaning of his book title as the black hole between data and knowledge.[11] Attacking this black hole and closing the gap between information and understanding are our greatest challenges and our greatest opportunities. We must find human understanding and wisdom in our vast warehouses of information, that is, in our libraries, for libraries are first and foremost information delivery systems.

In a book about the information age, coedited by Jennifer Slack of Florida Atlantic University, the following paragraph appears: "Millions of telephones, thousands of minicomputers, and miles of optical fiber will not create a golden age of . . . information. . . . People always dream about a better future, and our social system encourages this imaginative dreaming. The information society is one such social dream . . . when discussing a possible better future, we must argue in social, not primarily technological terms. To make that future a reality we must act in social, not technological terms."[12]

That means people shaping the future, not technologies shaping the future. I do not believe in technological predestination and find little evidence elsewhere to support such a view. For example, in a study (conducted for the NSF) of over one hundred information service innovations that failed to reach the marketplace, over 70 percent of the failures were attributed to factors other than technology, factors such as management, marketing, and finance.[13] For me, that study and my own experience indicates the need for an activist or interventionist model of change, not one of technological predestination, which I believe is far too passive a view.

It is not enough, not nearly enough, to wait for technology. We must embrace technology and use it to fulfill our goals; we must not let it dictate our goals.

Before I say more about goal setting, let me discuss briefly the conditions necessary for successful use of technology. Just as we have studies of the failure of innovation, we also have studies of the successful implementation of innovation. The findings of these studies point the way for us. They indicate the conditions necessary for success:

- There must be an understanding of the technology in terms of its advantages over other technologies already available. This understanding must include a thorough knowledge of costs and the relation to processes already in use.

- Feasibility demonstrations are necessary but not sufficient. Such demonstrations help to identify shortcomings and give early warning signals where improvements are needed.

- Advocates or champions are needed among both the producers and the user groups to ensure that early obstacles do not become permanent barriers.

- External pressures, such as competition and other threats, help to stimulate the implementation process.

- Joint programs involving multiple organizations provide a broader base of support for the innovation in its early stages.

- Availability of adequate capital is essential and must not be taken for granted. Ideas do not sell themselves; they require constant attention, and that requires capital.

- Visibility of consequences is a strong motivator to avoid failure. Announcing publicly an objective makes it more difficult to turn away from that objective.

- Social support is often a key element and may involve organizations that can provide moral, if not financial, support.

- Promotional agents such as the press or other public relations groups can help to ensure that all affected parties understand the technology and how it will benefit them. Such agents also help to elevate the visibility of consequences (see above).[14]

These factors lead me to a model for change that incorporates bridges. The model for change involves two types of bridges between the present and the desired future. First is a retrospective bridge (call it feedback) that compares what we said we wanted with what we have accomplished thus far (that is, accountability). Second is a forward-acting bridge that is based on intervention, or making the future develop according to our wishes, not someone else's. What ties these two bridges together (accountability and intervention) are an analysis of our successes and failures and a sharing of our experience openly with one another (as I quoted at the outset). We need to learn how to create learning organizations, that is, organizations that treat every effort, every group, every program as an opportunity to share experience and to learn from that experience.

New Technologies for Information Delivery

In 1985 the Library Network at AT&T developed a new approach for service delivery, a physical facility called an information access station. For those of you in the public library sector, it was not unlike a minibranch library. In fact, it was housed in a Portastructure™ enclosure of about three hundred square feet. The purpose of this venture was to learn about new approaches to delivering information services to an audience accustomed to equating level of service with size of physical facility. The access station provided a combination of physical, electronic, and human resources to our customers at a unit cost (and in a space) far less than that of previous traditional libraries. The design built upon ideas used in the banking industry: Deliver basic service via electronics, go where the customer is, give a human interface where needed, and rely on networking for service support. We have installed six access stations with more to come. We have learned much about change in the process. The design for this innovation was published in the 1987 *Special Library Association Journal,*[15] and many of our findings have been presented subsequently at professional meetings.

The access station uses only proven off-the-shelf technologies and draws upon resources already available elsewhere in the network. It is a means of moving service closer to the patron's work place. If this sounds familiar, it should. The banking scenario I painted earlier is a direct model for the information access station concept. The information access station provides the following functions:

- Access to current journals in hardcopy on site.
- Access to key works, including reference material and selected books for local circulation only.
- Access to local databases by terminals or microcomputers with user friendly front-end software.
- Access to remote databases offered by commercial vendors as well as central AT&T databases with user-friendly front-end software and downloading software.
- Access to back copies of journals and other normally space intensive material stored on high-density storage media. Currently, this media is microform but will soon include optical disk technology.
- Access to holdings of other sources via bibliographic utilities, such as OCLC, and via a union catalog of holdings within AT&T. Access in

this sense includes the ability to transmit facsimiles or request hardcopies via slower delivery mechanisms.

- Access to human interaction with an on-site staff member who is a trained generalist in the areas of marketing or cross-selling of services, training of users, and generalized reference service.

- Access to expert assistance by means of telephone or electronic mail in specialized reference areas.

- Access from the client's own workstation by means of a special electronic mail interface and online database services for selected functions listed above (e.g., local and remote database access, expert reference assistance).

The key point I want to make here is that the access station was as much a learning vehicle for change as it was a service delivery innovation. I'd like to turn now to a second example drawn from AT&T's Library Network. Just as we are using the access station concept to extend the physical presence of our network without adding costly library facilities, we are using electronic systems to extend the virtual presence of our network. AT&T has over four thousand buildings in its domain. Less than 3 percent of these buildings have populations of five hundred people or more. We need to deliver services to AT&T professionals regardless of their location, and we certainly cannot build libraries in all those buildings with less than five hundred people. So we are relying more and more on electronic interfaces for information searching, document ordering and information delivery. We now have over ten thousand active online users who generate eighteen to twenty thousand sessions per month. We are adding over fifty new users per week and reaching internationally to AT&T locations throughout the world. We provide access to over twenty-five internally developed databases that provide document request and in some cases full-text capability.

A second remote batch order entry system built around an electronic-mail facade provides users with access to our services via their own local machines. With this service they can submit database searches, order in-house documents or external photocopies, request library books or purchase books, submit reference requests, and request log-in access to our real-time interactive database systems. In many cases responses are in a matter of minutes for database searches, so it is almost real time. Even so, with a total potential market of over one hundred thousand professionals, we have a market penetration for our on-line real-time services of 10 percent. If we add the second remote batch electronic-mail-based service to this figure, our penetration jumps to 20 percent; if we include all use of our network, including physical access, the figure is 30 percent. So we still have much to do to effectively market our services to all our customers and to reduce unit costs by increasing our service base.

The Two Philosophies of Information Service

I realize I am talking in business terms when I discuss market penetration, total potential market and unit costs. I believe we must embrace not only such terminology but also the underlying philosophy of business if we are to survive and, better still, thrive in today's environment. For we operate in a competitive environment where scarce resources are allocated by decision makers on the basis of perceived value. As library leaders, we need not only a dedication to the services we provide but also a willingness to compete for resources on the same terms as other information–oriented organizations. I can assure you that computing centers learned long ago to understand the unit costs of their services and to argue in terms of return on investment. We must do the same. This, I believe, will require us to challenge the most fundamental philosophies of leadership in our profession.

We recently funded a study of the value of our services with King Research, Inc. This study showed a return-on-investment of between 400 and 1000 percent (in line with office automation results, but still so high that many managers don't believe the real leverage of information). In the public sector you could expect the same return from an effective literacy program, considering the social cost of an illiterate child growing to be an illiterate adult.

Lord Kelvin said, ". . . when you can measure what you are speaking about and express it in numbers, you know something about it, but when you cannot express it in numbers, your knowledge is of a meagre and unsatisfactory kind. . . ."[16] We cannot afford meager knowledge in today's environment.

I believe there are two basic philosophies of information service leadership. First is the traditional view that information organizations are institutions providing service of immeasurable value. Second is the view that any information service/product has a measurable value. These are two fundamentally incompatible philosophies, and I believe library leaders must make a choice in order to preserve their institutions in the evolving information-oriented society of today.

Let's look more closely at these two philosophies. In the immeasurable-value approach, organizations are justified on qualitative assertions. Resources required are quantified (budgets), but output measures are deemphasized. Instead value is measured by volumes held or size of budget. The link between mission and output is subjective, and productivity is not (and cannot be) measured. Budgets are incremental, and accountability focuses on resources used.

2 Basic Philosophies

In the measured-value approach, organizations are justified by quantitative assertions (i.e., improved productivity by 20 percent, achieved ROI of 35 percent, decreased illiteracy by 20 percent). Resources required are quantified, but so are output and productivity. The link between mission and output is objective, and budgets are programmatic where decisions are made on basis of program benefits. Accountability focuses on input and output measures.

This second approach has serious implications for the infrastructure of your organization. It moves your library and its services into the mainstream of the broader community in which you reside. It positions the library as a delivery mechanism, rather than as a warehouse, with an emphasis on output, not assets. It moves the library leader closer to key decision makers who understand this type of quantification. It also increases the potential for power struggles (every benefit has its cost).

Consistent with this second philosophy is the idea that every library should have a clear mission, a clear vision, a set of goals and objectives, and the strategies needed to achieve those goals and objectives with measurable results. This means that planning must be part of your standard operating environment.

The Business Planning Process

The following is a description of the various components of the business planning process adapted from Leza and Placericia.[17]

An organizational analysis includes understanding the history, purpose, and key players within your organization. Significant events, current structure and staffing, historical and current trends in funding and service levels, current new service plans, and current and new user groups to be served must also be studied. Take into account your organization's strengths and weaknesses. Are any technologies used or planned? Compare the organization's costs with those of similar institutions. Understand what resources are required to provide services.

A competitive analysis of other sources for similar services is essential. What are the advantages of your institution and your competitors? Rate competitors as strong, average, or weak.

Using a market analysis, take into account the geographic scope of users served and the demographics of the users. How can they be segmented (by life style, economics, etc.)? What distribution channels are used? What promotional strategies are employed? Also analyze the volume of services delivered, the rate of growth of services, and the share of market served by you versus your competitors.

Strategy setting for specific long-term objectives is also important. This includes performance indicators to measure objective achievement. What are the assumptions? Which strengths can be exploited? Are there weaknesses to overcome? Risks? Set specific strategies to be used involving technology, users, services, operations, finances, and back-up alternatives.

A management analysis identifies key functions and personnel responsible for each area (public relations, service promotion, etc.). The financial analysis should include a profit-and-loss statement, a balance sheet, and a break-even analysis. The profit-and-loss statement is a detailed description of revenue (from grants, taxes, sale of services) and operating expenses. The balance sheet lists all assets and liabilities. A break-even analysis will show fixed and variable costs versus revenues for various levels of service.

Monitoring results is also crucial. Compare results to commitments made in the business plan and adjust accordingly. Report results in an annual report comparing objectives to achievements. As an example, we publish an annual report of our activities that looks very much like a corporate annual report.

Conclusion

You should be developing an integrated set of short- and long-term plans that define your own future rather than have it defined for you. These plans should all be congruent with your mission – what you are about, your bridge to the rest of the organization – and with your vision – how you wish to evolve, or your own self-generated future definition. As an example, our mission at AT&T is to provide technical, business, and marketplace information needed by individuals and groups throughout AT&T at competitive cost. Our vision, which is our own definition of our future, is "to provide all professional employees throughout AT&T with an electronic window to the vast array of internal and external information services and to assure that the underlying information resources are managed as strategic assets providing a competitive advantage to AT&T." These two concepts together – what we do (our mission) and what we wish to be (our vision) – give us the direction to proceed.

Ah, but you say, I'm not in charge. I'm not the leader. That's not so. I believe that leadership resides anywhere in an organization where there are people with the passion and zeal to take up a vision and to follow that vision to make something happen. The truth is, most effective leaders are servants first. They are servants to their customers, servants to their institutions, and, most important, servants to their vision.

My personal vision as director of libraries and information systems and as current president of ASIS is that we will have leaders of libraries and other information services who are willing not only to be measured in terms of the value their activities contribute but also to be active in developing those measures. We must learn to compete in the arenas of power for resources, recognition, and, most important, for responsibility and key roles in the future. Otherwise, we lose to others, who, as Lewis Branscomb said, "fail to serve humanity as imaginatively and profoundly"[18] as we could.

At one time, we believed that over one-half of our U.S. work force consisted of knowledge workers. While inspiring, it was misleading. True knowledge workers may be far fewer than we believe and far fewer than necessary for the challenges we face. We need individuals willing to attack the human barrier to understanding, and they must understand that this is fundamentally a social challenge. Further, as leaders, we must understand that accountability (and a willingness to be held accountable) is essential.

In the new book entitled *Ideas and Information – Managing in a High-Tech World* (by AT&T's vice-president of research, Arno Penzias), Dr. Penzias writes, "As I see it, a healthy flow of information separates winning organizations from losers."[19] Note that the emphasis is on information flow, not storage. For us to lead winning organizations, we must place our emphasis on service delivery, that is, on information flow, not on accumulation of resources.

Notes

1. F. W. Lancaster, *Libraries and Librarians in the Age of Electronics* (Arlington, Va.: Info Resource Press, 1982), 150.

2. R. E. Lucier and J. F. Dooley, "Cosmology and the Changing Role of Libraries: An Analogy and Reflections," *Journal of the American Society for Information Science* 36, no. 1 (January 1985): 47.

3. P. Battin, "National and International Perspectives" [Paper presented at the Library and Information Resources for the Northwest (LIRN) Advisory Committee Meeting, 31 July 1984].

4. L. M. Branscomb, "The Electronic Library," *Journal of Communication* 31, no. 1 (Winter 1981): 150.

5. *Alliance for Excellence: Librarians Respond to a Nation at Risk* (U.S. Department of Education, available from U.S. Government Printing Office, July 1984), 45.

6. R. Brautigan, *The Abortion: An Historical Romance 1966* (New York: Simon and Schuster, 1971), 20.

7. D. H. Wilson, "Critical Mass: The Growth of the Information Industry," *Information Times,* August 1987.

8. *Information Industry Bulletin* 4, no. 1 (7 January 1987): 3.

9. National Commission on Libraries and Information Science, "An NCLIS Library Statistical Sampler," *Library Journal* 15 (October 1985): 35-38.

10. H. Becker, "Can Users Really Absorb Data at Today's Rates? Tomorrow's?" *Data Communications,* July 1986, 177-93.

11. R. S. Wurman, *Information Anxiety* (New York: Doubleday, 1989).

12. L. Qvortrup, "The Information Age: Ideal and Reality," in *The Ideology of the Information Age,* ed. J. D. Slack and F. Fejes (Norwood, N.J.: Ablex Publishing Co., 1987), 133-45.

13. E. E. Sweezy and J. H. Hopper, "Obstacles to Innovation in the Scientific and Technical Information Services Industry" (Final report to the National Science Foundation from the Institute for Public Administration, Washington, D.C., IPA Monograph 76-2, October 1975).

14. K. Cohen, S. Keller, and D. Streeter, "The Transfer of Technology from Research to Development," *Research Management* 22 (May 1979): 11-17; J. M. Dutton and W. H. Starbuck, "Diffusion of an Intellectual Technology" (Paper presented at the Conference on Communication and Control in Social Processes, sponsored by the American Society for Cybernetics and the University of Pennsylvania, 1 November 1974).

15. W. D. Penniman, "Tomorrow's Library Today," *Special Libraries* 78 (Summer 1987): 195-205.

16. W. Thomson (Lord Kelvin), *Popular Lectures and Addresses* (New York: Macmillan, 1889), 73.

17. R. L. Leza and J. F. Placencia, *Develop Your Business Plan* (Sunnyvale, Calif.: Oasis Press, 1982).

18. Branscomb, "The Electronic Library."

19. A. Penzias, *Ideas and Information, Managing in a High-Tech World* (New York: W. W. Norton & Co., 1989).

Part 1
Reference Services for Today and Tomorrow

Traditional Reference Services in Today's Library

ANDREW M. HANSEN
Executive Director
Reference and Adult Services Division
American Library Association
Chicago, Illinois

Having a reasonably good memory has been a source of pride to me. It has given me a degree of confidence in dealing with less fortunate colleagues, and it has been useful at those times when I have been posted at the reference desk. A retentive memory is one attribute of a successful reference librarian.

Fortunately for my emotional well-being, my memory functions on a selective basis, although sometimes it is not selective enough, as in the case of my first reference disaster. I wish I could forget it. While an undergraduate, I worked as a page in the children's room of a city's main library. Under extreme emergency conditions, I sometimes was put in charge of the department during the lunch hour or the children's librarian's coffee break.

The fatal question came by telephone and had to do with a fairy tale. I neither knew the answer nor knew where to begin looking it up. There was no way I could put something in the caller's hands to occupy her and keep her off my back. Besides, I had not been to library school yet to learn that simple, useful technique. I was addled by the steady barrage that came my way, such as,"I am so-and-so and I write the 'Mary Lane' column. "(This was the local forerunner of "Dear Abby" and "Ann Landers.")" I need this information right away for a column I am doing for tomorrow's edition. I don't understand why you are so reluctant to help me." When I finally got off the phone and my supervisor returned from lunch, I gave her the details of this less than satisfactory encounter. I was told that so-and-so gave everyone a rough time, that I was not to feel bad, that the answer could be found in such and such a source, and that she would call so-and-so back. This incident strengthened my resolve not to become a librarian but to continue with my undergraduate math major, get a teaching certificate, and pursue a career of sharing the beauties of figures and shapes with high school students.

Reference Services in the Past

That incident happened about forty years ago. Reference service as we know it was still not long out of its incunabular period. James Wyer's book, *Reference Work*, the first textbook on reference service, published in 1930, was not quite twenty years old.

Writers on reference service all seem to credit Samuel Swett Green's 1876 *Library Journal* article, "Personal Relations Between Libraries and Readers," as the beginning of the modern era in reference service. In the twenty years following his paper, libraries began assigning staff members the responsibility to provide personal assistance to library users. The first full-time reference librarians were appointed in the late nineteenth century. In the library where I was a page were two librarians whose tenure dated back to the 1890s. Little did I know then that I was acquainted with the pioneers!

I do not propose to dwell on the history of the field, but I feel compelled to highlight the contributions of two seventeenth-century writers on librarianship who were ahead of their time and possibly ahead of some of our colleagues today.

Gabriel Naude wrote in 1627 in *Advice on Establishing a Library* that the librarian should:

- Take counsel with other librarians.
- Read everything written on books and bibliography.
- Put nonbook materials into the collection.
- See to it that the collection is used by all those who may have some need or use for the materials.

John Dury wrote a quarter of a century later. In his letters, known as the "Reformed Librarie-Keeper," he added to the librarian's responsibilities that of increasing published knowledge. When gaps existed in the library's collection and books could not be found to fill these gaps, then the librarian should promote an investigation by recognized scholars and help them in the production of new information resources. The librarian was to be a steward in the sources of learning and information.

The Role of the Reference Librarian

Perhaps you are wondering at this point whether I am going to attempt to define *traditional reference services.* I would rather not. Concern with definitions can be limiting. I would rather proceed along the line of the characters in Edith Wharton's short story "Xingu." The women in that story did not let their ignorance of Xingu stop them from discussing it completely.

As a public librarian twenty and thirty years ago, I worked with library-using adults, some of whom were the products of earlier library instruction programs. I formed a jaundiced opinion about those inadequate programs, which turned out people who thought they knew how to use a library because they knew all about the catalog and the *Reader's Guide.* They frequently did not know how to use the most important library resource, the reference librarian. They stopped me on the street or cornered me elsewhere in the community to complain because the library did not have information on whatever topic. When I responded with "Hadn't the reference librarian found something?" they said they had not asked. More recently I experienced one of those "aha" moments when I heard an academic reference librarian say that, as a result of the bibliographic instruction program on her campus, reference librarians were being approached with more significant reference questions than before. That this is seen as a mixed blessing is evidenced by a statement by an academic library administrator: "Unfortunately, too many libraries find that by teaching students to make better use of library resources, they have only increased the level of sophistication of demands, thus increasing the pressures for reference assistance and consultation."[1]

In its final report to the ALA council at the January 1989 midwinter Meeting in Washington, the ALA Presidental Committee on Information Literacy made several recommendations to the association, libraries, and other segments of the educational community on creating an information literate society, that is, preparing people for lifelong learning. In the words of the report, "To be information literate, a person must be able to recognize when information is needed and have the ability to locate, evaluate, and use effectively the needed information." That is, "Information literate people are those who have learned how to learn." Those bibliographic instruction students who have been taught by reference librarians how to make better use of the library's resources – human and material – are well on their way to becoming information literate.

The introduction to the reference and adult services division's landmark statement, "A Commitment to Information Services: Developmental Guidelines," cites the three levels of library-based activities that ensure the maximum use of information resources through substantive interaction with the users:

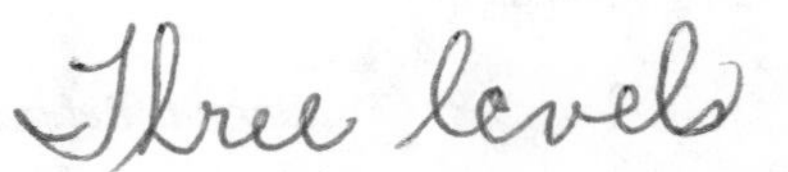

1. Reference or information services consisting of personal assistance to users in pursuit of information ranging from factual answers to single queries to extensive bibliographic searching.

2. Formal and informal instruction in the use of the library or information center and its resources, ranging from explanations of how to use individual library finding aids to formal courses.

3. Indirect reference service, which provides user access to informational sources and may extend the library's resources through interlibrary loan and other interagency cooperation activities such as referrals of questions rather than of questioners.

Although the introduction covers the range of levels, the text of the guidelines themselves is concerned almost entirely with reference or information services, that is, personal assistance to library users. Another way to describe this level of service is to call it liberal or maximum service, as contrasted with conservative or minimum service where the librarian points to the red book on the third shelf or asks "Have you looked in the catalog?" Moderate or middling service lies somewhere in between and may not vary so much from practitioner to practitioner as from one time to another, depending on how busy the reference department is, or what time of day it is, or when the reference librarian happens to be just plain lost on that day in what should be familiar surroundings.

Service by Appointment

Some writers in the field are questioning whether the reference desk is the appropriate meeting place for library user and librarian. The typical reference encounter may not be adequate for the help the user needs and may be too expensive to provide for the large number of directional questions dealt with in libraries. It is alleged that superior, in-depth service can be provided by reference librarians on an appointment basis.

Service by appointment is not a new concept in libraries. People with involved information needs have asked librarians to block out time to work with them, and beleaguered librarians have also asked clients to come back during quieter times. TV Telephone ads tell us to "call first," but I have yet to see and hear one of those telephone company ads focus on the library.

A short feature in the *Chicago Tribune* put it this way: "Life is regulated by appointments. Need a dentist? Phone for an appointment. A doctor, haircut, a permanent wave? You will need an appointment. etc., etc. . . . I'm waiting for the day shoppers will need an appointment to get into the checkout lane. Imagine phoning the library and asking when it would be convenient to withdraw a book."

Sometimes when a specific suggestion is developed, communication of it is inadequate and the message received is that it is a matter of all or nothing. I perceive this to be true in the discussions of information providing vesus bibliographic instruction. It is also true in discussions on the reference service by appointment versus that of the first-come, first-served basis; some of both is more likely to be the usual order of the day. If my barber shop can provide a combination of chairs available by appointment and chairs available on a first-come, first-served basis, why cannot the library's reference staff combine approaches to service? Are there any among us who have served at a reference desk who have not varied the level of service we have provided to different people based on our perceptions of their needs, our time available to work with them, and our own ability to cope with or our interest in the subject under consideration? In the section of the guidelines about ethics of service, we find that the type of question or status of user is not to be considered. Also, personal philosophies and attitudes should not be reflected in the execution of service or in the extent and accuracy of information provided.

Among ALA policies is one that asserts that the charging of fees and levies for information services, including those services utilizing the latest information technology, is discriminatory in publicly supported institutions providing library and information services. We need to be aware that there are risks "in changing these fees." In a recent article, Philip Whiteman, a British librarian, makes the point that British libraries have played a role in bringing on the financial problems they are currently facing. The doctrinaire political policies of their Conservative government concerning income generation, sponsorship, and privatism have found libraries' charges for service to be precedent setting. That libraries in Britain may be well on their way to becoming market-driven institutions is the message I read into his remarks.[2]

Accuracy of Information

Another concern in the provision of information is the matter of accuracy. A little more than twenty years ago, the Library Bill of Rights was amended by deletion of the phrase "of sound factual authority" as a qualifier for materials that should not be proscribed or removed from a library's collection. Ten years ago, when the RASD was amending "A Commitment to Information Services: Developmental Guidelines," the section on ethics of service was added. The matter of factual accuracy continued as an issue. The purists among reference librarians did not see accuracy as a matter of degree but as an absolute value. They said answers to questions *must* be accurate.

James Russell Lowell in his hymn "Once to Every Man and Nation" put the essential concept into these words:

New occasions teach new duties,
Time makes ancient good uncouth;
They must upward still and onward,
Who would keep abreast of truth.

Although neither the RASD board nor the ALA Intellectual Freedom Committee is a hymn-singing body, and indeed Lowell's hymn was not cited in the deliberations on ethics of service, a compromise on accuracy was reached in the statement, "Information provided the user in response to any inquiry must be the most accurate possible."

Jim Rettig, reviewer of reference works and frequent contributor to the literature of reference librarianship, described one of the problems of providing accurate information in his "In My Opinion" piece, "Love Canal in the Reference Stacks."[3] Rettig's concern in his editorial commentary was with outdated materials kept on the shelf and the potential harm the misinformation in them can do.

An example from my own experience of a minor problem along this line was the time I invited some colleagues on my staff to celebrate Danish Constitution Day with me. Three of us decided to look up some background information on the day and found three different years attached to June fifth as the day the constitution was signed by the Danish king. Investigation revealed that the country was then on its fourth constitution and that there was a tradition of having the king sign each new one on the same day as the first one had been signed. The books of days we consulted were published at widely varying times; each contained accurate information on the signing of the constitution in effect as of publication. None gave the historical background we located elsewhere. This experience has made me quite sympathetic to those who have been found to supply less than completely accurate answers to deceptively simple questions.

Guidance and Stimulation

Reference services in today's libraries include provision of information; instruction in the use of information resources, including the librarian; guidance in the selection of materials for programs of self-education and stimulation of the library's clientele to use the available human and material resources.

I have touched on provision of information and instruction in the use of libraries and information resources. Let me now turn to the topic of guidance. This aspect of reference service as I understand it relates to the library's program of service to adults, sometimes thought of as adult education programs, for the individual learner or for learners in groups. The readers' advisors of the 1920s and 1930s have long since disappeared from most libraries; the reference staff provides whatever help is given to people who seek to pursue informal learning programs on their own. Current awareness and selective dissemination of information programs as well as bibliotherapy fall in this area. Discussion groups and other programming endeavors are also included here.

A few months ago I participated in an adult education conference at which Swedish and American adult educators were present. I was the only librarian. It has been years now since I was challenged by anyone at an adult education meeting about the library's status as an agency for adult learning, but I have been. At this meeting I spoke with several Swedish adult educators who had never thought of their public libraries as adult education agencies. The consistent response was that Swedish libraries were organized as cultural institutions. I would like to think that some among them had an "aha" experience as a result of our conversations and went home to establish new liaisons that would accrue benefits to the providers and consumers of adult services in libraries and other adult education programs.

Margaret Monroe is given credit for identifying stimulation as one of the four fundamental functions of library public service. It does not stand by itself but both precedes and follows the other three (information, instruction, and guidance). Stimulation may take a variety of forms through public relations and the creation of a climate for use. Such things as signage, TV and radio announcements, book displays, film showings, community contacts, services to established groups, exhibits, informal conversations within and without the library, and participation of staff in local affairs are included. Stimulation prompts members of the library's community to use the library's resources. Stimulation following the use of information, instruction, or guidance is seen as the activation of the user. If a library's goal is to allow all citizens to realize and solve individual, social, and cultural needs, the realization of that goal will be cultural advancement and inclusiveness. Stimulation brings people to the library, and reference service provided liberally prepares them to act as a result of their library experience. In the Public Library Inquiry[4] of the late 1940s, librarians were seen as sharing the "library faith." Today that faith is seen in the information literacy movement.

The Traffic Officer

A columnist of yesteryear under the pen name of Simeon Stylites wrote a "Salute to Librarians"[5] in *The Christian Century.* He reported on a Philadelphia librarian who referred to himself as a traffic officer who arranged collisions between people and ideas. How better to describe the role of the active reference librarian, the provider of traditional reference service in today's library? The reference librarian who, as the situation warrants, provides specific information in response to queries, instructs the novice in the rules of information seeking, and guides the self-starter through intersections that are gridlocked, but for the librarian, with all kinds and qualities of media-containing information and ideas.

Notes

1. Joanne R. Euster, "Technology and Instruction," in *Bibliographic Instruction: The Second Generation,* (Littleton, Co.: Libraries Unlimited, 1987), 53-59.

2. Philip Whiteman, "The Library and Society: A New Look at Old Values," *Library Review* 37, no. 2, (1988): 7-18.

3. Janus Rettig, "Love Canal in the Reference Stacks," *Reference Services Review,* Winter 1982, 7.

4. Robert D. Leigh, *The Public Library in the United States: The General Report of the Public Library Inquiry* (New York: Columbia University Press, 1950).

5. "Salute to Librarians," *Christian Century,* 14 March 1956, 328.

Impact of Technology on Today's Reference Services

MICHAEL J. MCGILL
Vice President
Research and Technology Assessment and Development
OCLC Online Computer Library Center
Dublin, Ohio

When Dr. Trezza asked me to participate in this meeting, I felt uncomfortable for two reasons. First, I am not officially a trained librarian and thus have had no practical experience in dealing with the everyday tasks associated with reference activities. Second, he requested that I speak about the state of the art today. My job makes me responsible for research and development at the world's leading cataloging facility. While OCLC's services are often used in support of reference, today we have only a very few services that are directly reference services. My responsibility is to keep looking at the future and to build toward that future.

I accepted Dr. Trezza's kind invitation because of OCLC's movement toward helping to fulfill the information needs of the reference professional. This is in keeping with OCLC's charter which states that we are to "further the ease of access to and use of the ever expanding body of worldwide scientific, literary, and educational knowledge and information." I have a personal interest in information retrieval. Information must be available to individuals in support of their information needs.

Background

Reference activities is inherently an ill-defined concept; the immediate desire is for a definition of the service. My search was only partially futile – I did discover a quotation from Katz that states: "While there is more to Reference Services than answering questions, essentially that is the primary goal."[1]

This pretty well characterizes the existing field of reference services even if it is unfortunately broad. A more specific definition of reference services is those library and information services that are directed to the support of dissemination and use, rather than the acquisition or organization of information. The purpose of a reference service is usually to provide more direct patron service in answering queries, provide guidance in the information search, or provide the information. Attempts to accomplish these purposes have caused the creation of new or better information resources, better connection to information resources, better systems that give access to the resources, and better systems for the creation of documents. These will be considered later in this paper.

Reference services are provided by librarians to users and typically to those users who explicitly request these services. These users are self-selecting, are knowledgeable enough to know that the service is available, and have enough skill to be able to pursue the service. Reference service users have an above average education; their backgrounds have taught them to use the information they find; they are from the professional strata of the middle and upper middle income classes; and in general they can be characterized as information literate.[2] They use the information supplied for academic, business, scientific, government, and technological needs.

The information resources of today include the traditional printed resources, many of which are secondary services that point to information rather than provide a direct answer. Alos, computer services such as Dialog or the National Library of Medicine (NLM) have been available for about the past twenty years. Recently, local computerized services such as Online Public Access Catalogs (OPACs) and compact discs appeared. Changes have come, not primarily in content, but in media and access.

Finally, the nature of the information environment has changed from a print-oriented, information-poor environment to a multimedia information-glutted environment. Twenty years ago the person holding the information was in a powerful position. Today the person in power is the one who can find the relevant data among the vast quantities of materials that are readily available.

Today's Technological Environment

It is interesting to look at the most recent twenty years of change for clues to what the future will provide, but, as important, the changes help us to understand better why we are in the current environment and what people's expectations are for today.

Higher education as a whole provides a convenient framework for understanding these changes. According to Van Houweling, the goals of higher education are dependent on one's ability to create/acquire, store, retrieve, transmit, and use information. The library's role is the acquisition, storage, retrieval, and transmission of the information. In fact, as the repository of information items, it is no accident that one finds libraries at the symbolic center of many of the world's universities.[3]

During the past twenty years, the educational environment, and thus the library, have become increasingly dependent upon technology. In the case of the library, this dependency came about first when technology became a management tool for the vast resources of information items. (For example, circulation systems were developed to meet the need for collection control and management.) The tools of automation eventually were applied to the storage and retrieval of the information items. The premier example of this automation activity may well be OCLC. The Ohio College Library Center resulted from the concern of a number of individuals about the increasing costs of cataloging books and the realization that storing and retrieving cataloging information from a single database could result in a significant savings. This evolved into the Online Computer Library Center when it became clear that the resources its founders had created had value well beyond the state of Ohio.

Today one needs more than simple storage and retrieval; one expects to be able to actually use the information that is discovered. Usage may simply mean including citations in a bibliography such as that offered by Personal Bibliographic Systems (PBS), or, on the more complex side, it may mean directly incorporating tables, charts, and graphs into a published document. Libraries and specifically reference services have adapted to these changes by doing searches for users, creating bibliographies, training users to conduct searches, and occasionally maintaining databases.

The libraries are the users of technology. Seldom are they instigators or developers of technological change. The technology is perceived to be the responsibility of the computing center, the telecommunications officer, or in some instances a chief information officer. If one examines the computing technology over the past twenty years, then one sees the growth of a modest activity into a large organization with a budget that rivals and, in some cases, exceeds that of the library. The computing technologies originally focused on data but now focus on information and uses such as scholars' workstations. That is, there has been convergence. This is best exemplified by Columbia University, which was among the first to bring the library and computing together. They are now joined by Carnegie-Mellon University, Vanderbilt University, and probably many others.

The changes that have occurred in technology are phenomenal. The cost-effectiveness of information technology increased by a factor of one thousand between 1950 and 1980, and this rate of increase is expected through at least the year 2000. To put this in perspective, if a technological item cost one million dollars in 1950, that same item will cost ten dollars in the year 2000. Van Houweling notes that "Information Technology will continue to improve in cost-effectiveness for the foreseeable future at a rate at least comparable to the recent past.[4]

One of the areas that is changing most rapidly is the telecommunications environment. Although the breakup of AT&T caused a great deal of change, the most dramatic change for the reference professional will come from the use of technology through facilities like the NSFnet. NSFnet is a network established by the National Science Foundation to support research in the United States. The network grew out of the 1985 super computer initiative at the foundation. It was eventually separated from the super computer initiative and has taken on its own separate and important existence. The importance of the networking activity, as defined by NSF officials, is to:

- Support collaborative research efforts through:

    More effective knowledge dissemination.

    Faster results.

    More equitable involvement in large research projects.

    Qualitative enhancement of research.

- Provides access to remote research facilities.
- Provides access to centralized scientific information.
- Provides access to computer systems.
- Allows control of remote experimental facilities.

The network is organized in a three-level hierarchy, starting with a backbone that is managed by the MERIT consortium in Michigan in cooperation with MCI and IBM. This feeds and is fed by a series of regional networks such as SURANET and NYSERNet. These in turn are connected to campus networks or consortia of campus networks.[5] The connectivity that is provided by these networks gives one the potential of a great deal of information exchange. This is made clear when one considers the plans for the capacity of the network. Fig. 1 shows a plan for a 1.5 megabit-per-second capacity in 1988–89. This has been achieved. The plan then calls for a 45 megabit capacity in 1991–92, and a 3 gigabit capacity in 1994–95. The plan, if successful, will allow a full compact disc of information to be transmitted in less than a second. A remaining problem is that one cannot get the data off the disc fast enough to use that capacity. More important, it means that documents with color, graphics, and even motion can be transmitted in real time. Three gigabits will still be a limitation to some of the high energy physicists, but to the reference professional it will represent the removal of any significant barrier in moving information. That is, the capacity will be present, and it will be economical and at least in part government subsidized. However, it will not be tuned or developed for the library reference information applications. Rather, it will test the ingenuity of the library and information science community to take this resource and turn it into a valuable tool for scientists, scholars, students, and others. As a start, both OCLC and RLG are working to make their reference resources available on this network.

Figure 1. Timetable for National Research Network

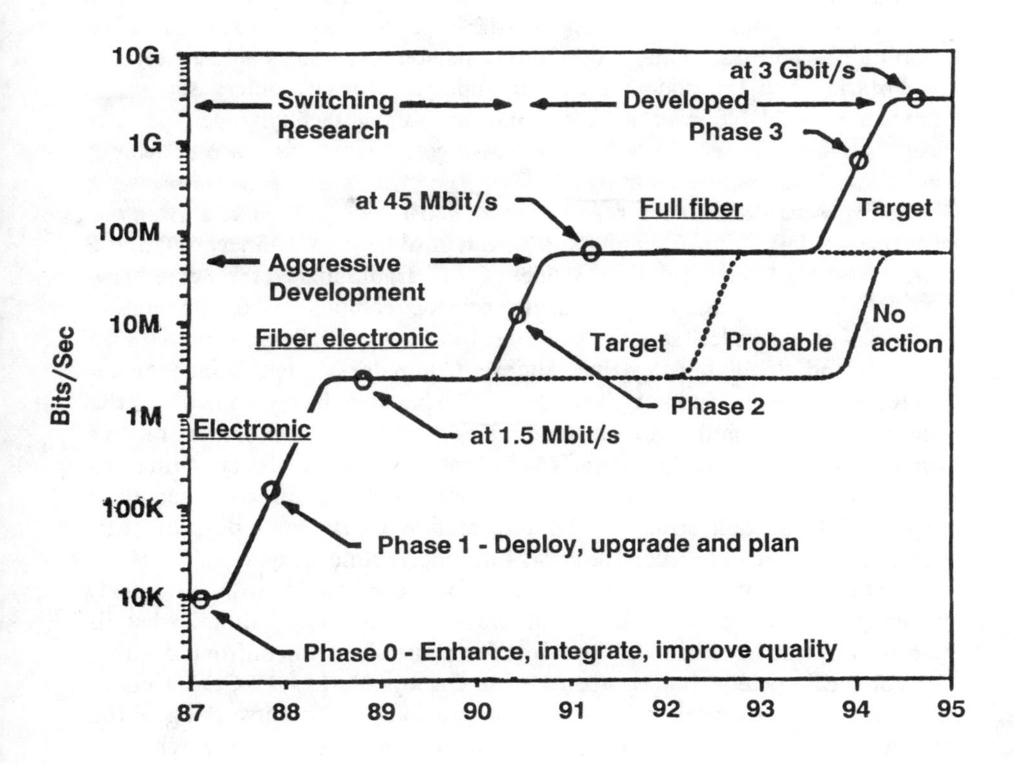

The ability to store vast quantities of information will not be covered in detail in this paper because it is a very prevalent discussion topic among the library and information community. It is simply noted that storage density is increasing dramatically. Advances come from a variety of sources and need to be followed carefully and evaluated objectively. As one example, it is rumored that there will be a compact disc with four times the density of current available discs. OCLC is working to validate its existence, determine its reliability and performance, determine the impact on existing equipment and resources including mastering facilities, and finally determine the benefit of a technology such as this in the context of the many other technological changes that are occurring. Regular magnetic disks with a gigabyte of storage already exist, and disks that use vertical magnetic storage have density approaching or exceeding optical storage. Fig. 2 shows the technological environment that we believe we must understand in order to continue to make significant advances in products and services for our members.

Implications for the Reference Library

The library has become part of the overall information technology environment. There have been fundamental changes in the way librarians serve clients. Consider the way in which people acquire and preserve information. The traditional mode, direct person-to-person contact between the librarian and the client, is still operational. However, increasingly the librarian is available over an electronic messaging facility. Questions get asked, searches are conducted, answers are given, documents are delivered, and gratitude is expressed without face-to-face or even voice communication. Increasingly the information resources are distributed. That is, it is often the case that a scholar or the scholar's department will own a compact disc and a workstation that are located outside of the traditional reference library domain. It is increasingly popular to provide campus-based information systems. For example, Georgia Tech has installed BRS/Search software on campus and loaded Magazine Index, Computer Index, Management Contents, Trade and Industry, and INSPEC. These are freely available to the students, faculty, and staff of Georgia Tech. Once a member of this community has identified an item, a request is made of the library to find and define the item for the individual. The Georgia Tech librarians see their responsibility as delivering all the information to the members of their community and readily accept requests for document delivery.

The reference profession is therefore confronted with a quickly changing technological environment where expectations about what is possible are well established. The reference professional is confronted with a technological society that competes with Disney World's EPCOT Center. The collaboration among scientists made possible by the networking of the nation and the campuses is also enhancing applications research. For

Figure 2. Developing Technologies

DEVELOPING TECHNOLOGIES — 1988 September 15

(Timeline axis: 1970, 1980, 1990)

Processor Technologies	Mainframes; Minis; Micros; Fault Tolerant; Supermicros; Commercial Database Machines; Symbolic Processors (LISP Machines); Specialized Text-Search Processors; Highly Parallel Processors; Transputer; 5th Generation (Non-Traditional Arch.); Optical Computers
Mass Storage Technologies	Magnetic Tape/Disk; Floppy Disk; Winchester Disk; Video Disk; Optical Disk; Optical Card; Optical Film; Digital Audio Tape (DAT); Erasable Optical; Digital Paper; Photon-Gated Materials
Person Machine Interface	Menu/Command; "User Friendly"; Icons; Pulldown Menus; Common Command Language; Specialized Expert Systems; Some Natural Language
Input	Keyboard; Joysticks; Light Pen; Touch Screen; Mouse; OCR; Some Voice/Input; High Resolution Scanners; Larger Vocabulary Voice Input/ (Speaker Dependent); Intelligent OCR; Large Vocabulary Voice Input/ (Speaker Independent)
Output	Monochrome Alpha Displays; Low Resolution Graphics; Color; High Resolution Graphics; Windowing; Voice; Laser Printers; Character LCD; Personal Copiers/Printers; Portable High Resolution Reflection Monitor; Hologram/Output
Workstations	Intelligent Terminals; Stand Alone Processors; CAD/CAM Workstations; Personal Computer Workstations; LISP Machines; Personal Super Computers; Intelligent Information Appliances
Software	Specialized Modular Development Design; Structured Design; Programming Development Tools; Software Engineering; Application Generators; Development Environments; Very High Level Languages; Integrated CASE Tools
Telecommunications	Terrestrial (Twisted Pairs, COAX, Microwave); Satellite; Packet Networks; Fiber Optics; Local Area Networks; Divestiture; Bypass; Cellular; Metropolitan Area Networks; Packet Radio; ISDN; Space Platform
Applications	Algorithm-IC (Batch/Some Interactive); Some Heuristics; Intelligent Networking; Some Expert Systems; Knowledge-based Programs; Machine Translation; Hypermedia-based Systems; Process of Non-Text for Retrieval

example, artificial intelligence work has brought about expert systems in the field of medicine, petroleum exploration, nuclear reactor management, and even some library fields.

The wired campus has become a reality. Unfortunately, the reference professional is confronted with a situation in which the wiring of the campus often went ahead without a well-established plan for the information resources that the wired campus will support. This information resource planning is now beginning to occur. Projects to develop prototypes of future environments are being established. A good example is Project Mercury, which is a joint activity between Carnegie-Mellon University and OCLC.

The goal of Mercury is to build a prototype electronic library that will serve as a laboratory for research. The scholar will have access to full documents, an intelligent assistant that will aid in the search process, a capability to convert documents directly from paper into machine-readable documents, and indexing that is enhanced by natural language understanding. The machine-readable documents will have not only the text but also the same type font as the original typesetting information images, including charts and graphs. The goal is to provide the user with a full electronic library at a workstation. This is very similar to the goal of Project INTREX carried out at MIT in the 1960s. The significant difference is that the infrastructure is now in place to support the project.

The Mercury project is in its first phase. The search engine from OCLC's EPIC product is being moved to the campus environment to operate under Unix. A strategy for handling image as well as full text will build from OCLC's Graph Text system, and an initial collection of artificial intelligence information is being constructed. The project will then move to porting a peer-to-peer interface for information retrieval (Z39.50) into this environment, developing a window-based interface. The system will then grow to a large multigigabyte environment. Substantial research capabilities will then be undertaken within the prototype.[6] For example, studies of user behavior, economies, and system performance and capabilities will be supported by the environment.

The clear message to the reference professional is that today's reference environment is significantly more challenging than in recent years. An understanding of technology is mandatory. One's ability to provide an answer to a question is enhanced by access and impeded by the vast quantities of information that can be readily found. The technology will continue to become less expensive. The users of information resources are more knowledgeable and have higher expectations of the results. Users want improvements in access through subject searching, deeper insight into the information content of the item, additional information about the location of the item and its availability, and access to many different kinds of materials.[7]

The world of the reference professional is different now than it was even ten years ago. Much of this change has been driven by technological change. The rate of change of technological innovation continues to increase. One must conclude that this will cause even greater changes in the reference environment over the next ten years.

Notes

1. William A. Katz, *Introduction to Reference Work*, vol. 1, *Basic Information Source* (New York: McGraw Hill, 1987), 3.

2. William A. Katz, *Introduction to Reference Work*, vol. 2, *Service and Reference Processes* (New York: McGraw Hill, 1987), 4.

3. Douglas E. Van Houweling, "The Information Technology Environment of Higher Education," in *Campus of the Future Conference in Information Resources* (Dublin, Ohio: OCLC Online Computer Library Center, 1987), 59-106.

4. Ibid.

5. Personal communication with Bill Wolf of the National Science Foundation in 1988.

6. *The Mercury Electronic Library* (Carnegie-Mellon University, February 1989).

7. Lynne Brindley, "The Future of the OPACs: An Academic Library Perspective," in *OPACs and Beyond*, Proceedings of a Joint Meeting of the British Library, DBMIST, and OCLC, 17-18 August 1988 (Dublin, Ohio: OCLC, 1989), 57-66.

Changing Technology and Tomorrow's Reference Services

THOMAS J. GALVIN
Executive Director
American Library Association
Chicago, Illinois

About three years ago, the Information Industry Association, a trade organization made up chiefly of private sector information vendors, commissioned a study by the Institute for Alternative Futures of Alexandria, Virginia.[1] The authors, Clement Bezold and Robert Olson, identified and described four alternative scenarios for the year 2000, now only a decade away. Two of those scenarios – respectively named "things bog down" and "1984 and beyond" – are highly pessimistic. The negative scenarios envision a failure on the part of society to capitalize on advances in information technology in a way that improves the general quality of life. A third option termed "the high-tech information society" simply assumes continuation of the economic trends that have characterized the 1970s and the 1980s – boom times for the information industry – and predicts a marketplace model of information access in which the gap between the "information haves" and the "information have-nots" continues to grow with each successive technological enhancement.

It is Bezold and Olson's fourth option for the year 2000 that at once captures our imagination as information professionals and provides the optimistic title for their study, *The Information Millenium.* The information millenium, in turn, is characterized by what the authors term "the creative society." They describe the creative society as one that "assumes rapid

technological progress and a dynamic economy." In this scenario, however, they write, "The Information Revolution combines with a profound change in values: more expressive, socially concerned values lead to a recognition that human creativity is the heart of the Information Revolution." In their vision of the creative society, "Home information use grows even faster than the GNP." "Public libraries flourish . . . and make massive amounts of information widely available."[2]

For these authors, the key to which outcome will prevail is not success in achieving major technological breakthroughs in the laboratory but rather the successful identification and effective resolution of information policy options in the political arena. Indeed, they observe, "If we can avoid pitfalls, like the misuse of information technology for social control, then current developments have the potential to converge towards what might be called universal information access."[3]

Establishing Information Literacy

Universal information access is, it seems to me, the proper and achievable goal of reference and information service. Even beyond universal access is the ability to bring information resources effectively to bear on fundamental human information needs. This, in turn, requires major reform and redirection of the educational process to raise the general level of information literacy.

Bezold and Olson's information industry study characterizes the information literacy problem in these terms, "The key issue facing our society is the creativity gap: tremendous information resources now exist to stimulate creativity and social problem-solving, but the average person knows little about them."[4] Working independently, and in a rare instance of agreement between two organizations that usually find themselves on opposite sides of most public issues, a special Presidential Committee of the American Library Association earlier this year issued a landmark report on the critical state of information literacy. "Information," the ALA committee observes, "is expanding at an unprecedented rate, and enormously rapid strides are being made in the technology for storing, organizing and accessing the ever-growing tidal wave of information." However, the expansion of information resources has not served to raise the general level of information access. Instead, as the ALA committee points out, "The combined effect of these factors is an increasingly fragmented information base – large components of which are only available to people with money and/or acceptable institutional affiliations."[5]

To achieve broader information equity, the American Library Association believes that information professionals must join forces with educators at all levels, from preschool through graduate school, to produce a new generation of information literates, persons who, in the words of the

Presidential Committee, are "able to recognize when information is needed and have the ability to locate, evaluate and use effectively the needed information."[6] In April 1989, in Washington, D.C., ALA's American Association of School Librarians joined with the National Commission on Libraries and Information Science to convene a high-level invitational conference, bringing librarians together with educational leaders to begin to forge a new national coalition on information literacy.

Let me be careful here to distinguish between information literacy and what is commonly called computer literacy. Computer literacy is much too narrow and limiting for the concept I am trying to express. Certainly, understanding how to communicate with and how to direct computing machines is embodied in the concept of information literacy, but information literacy encompasses far more than merely learning how to create and execute programs, how to run standard statistical packages, or how to query a remote database. It certainly does incorporate understanding how to use the computer as a communication and information-gathering device. Beyond that, it is understanding the range, variety, and specific characteristics of remote databases. Information literacy means mastery of the software capabilities required to tap into those databases, to merge portions of them, to download relevant portions, and to manipulate and reformat those data to meet one's specific, individual informational need.

Most important of all, to my mind, information literacy involves the capacity to access and to make effective use of the *full range* of information resources, *both print and electronic,* both public files and private databases. Information literacy, as I define it, also involves understanding how and when to call upon trained information professionals to help in the process of formulating an information need in a manner that produces optimal response from a given set of information resources. A key professional role, then, becomes that of matching an individual's information need to the best available configuration of information resources, irrespective of their location or their format.

In short, what I am proposing as a fundamental component of basic education is at once to broaden the traditional notion of computer literacy and to merge it with the long-established concept of bibliographic instruction. The goal should be to develop in *every individual* the capacity to mobilize effectively the full range of informational resources, irrespective of format or location, that are relevant to a given information need.

Moving from Document Delivery to Information Transfer

Pursuit of the goal of universal information access will require both the creation of an information literate society and a redefinition by librarians of the nature of the reference process. In particular, I believe that our profession will need to distinguish very clearly between document delivery on the one hand and information transfer on the other. Indeed, I suggest to you that modern information technology now provides us with both the opportunity and the obligation to transform the basic mission of the library from one of document delivery into one of information transfer.

Information transfer is, at once, a broader, more inclusive term than document delivery and a much higher order process. In assessing what occurs at the reference desk, even now we seemingly continue to assume either that document delivery is synonymous with information transfer or that information transfer follows from document delivery in some fashion that is not ordinarily the professional concern of the librarian. We most commonly behave professionally as though the proper domain of librarianship does not in fact extend very far at all beyond the boundaries of document delivery.

Redefining the Library

Given the significantly higher level of reference and information service that technology increasingly places within our professional grasp, I suggest that it will no longer be enough for the library to define success simply in terms of being able to place a needed document in the hands of a library user in timely fashion. The library will, I believe, need to be able to do substantially more for people than just to make them happy bibliographically. In short, it seems to me essential for our profession to be about the business of establishing new norms and new standards for reference and information services that are responsive and appropriate to the enhanced capabilities that new technology has placed at our disposal.

I believe that the formulation and definition of new, higher level information service goals will be essential if libraries are to retain a central role as an integrative force in building an informed society. To continue to compete successfully for increasingly scarce financial resources, libraries must be in a position to offer their constituents something beyond simply more of the same. Stephen Muller, president of Johns Hopkins University, poses the challenge to academic librarians in these terms:

> "What I see is a drastic change in the nature of what we mean by learning, in the way in which learning is conveyed and in the impacts which the new communications and information technologies will have on the university. I see a persistent drive on the part of the institution to adjust to those changes and to recover some coherence. In all of that, the library has the opportunity to become the major university communications center. Otherwise, librarians can define themselves as museum archivists, and continue to nurture and to guard the printed book, paying no attention to these other things."[7]

The ALA Committee on Information Literacy offers, eight years later, a similar challenge to public libraries. The committee observes that:

Communication Center (or)

Museum archivist — no progress

> "Libraries, which provide a significant public access point to . . . information and usually at no cost, must play a key role in preparing people for the demands of today's information society. Just as public libraries were once a means of education and a better life for many of over twenty million immigrants of the late 1800s and early 1900s, they remain today as the potentially strongest and most far-reaching community resource for lifelong learning. Public libraries not only provide access to information, but they also remain crucial to providing people with the knowledge necessary to make meaningful use of existing resources. They remain one of the few safeguards against information control by a minority."[8]

One potential constraint on our collective enthusiasm for and commitment to the information literacy concept may be a concern that, as clients become more self-sufficient in brokering their own information needs, aided by increasingly user-cordial retrieval systems, the role of the library and/or the role of the librarian might be significantly diminished. Indeed, such highly regarded visionaries as Professor Wilfred Lancaster have predicted the decline of the library as more and more of society's information resources become available in electronic form. "In the longer term," Lancaster asserted some six years ago, "it seems certain that the library will be bypassed" as users develop the ability to access electronic information sources from their homes. Lancaster offers greater hope for the future of the librarian, however, observing that "the librarian could long outlive the library." "In an age of electronics," he suggests, "we may need 'electronic librarians.'"[9]

Lancaster's warning serves a useful purpose in urging that professional education should focus more on developing the skills of the information intermediary and less on the institutional context in which those skills have traditionally been practiced. Clearly, as the Arthur D. Little firm predicted in 1981, "Between now and the year 2000, the idea of a 'library' as defined by LOCATION OR PLACE will continue to give way at an accelerating pace to the idea of a library . . . as ACCESS NETWORKS."[10]

Indeed, there is growing evidence that this is happening, especially in those academic environments where personal computers are widely available to faculty and students. Harvey Wheeler's provocative essay on "the virtual library" carries this notion to its logical conclusion, describing an academic environment in which both the library and the university are transformed into "a vast electronic knowledge processing system."[11]

Redefining the Role of the Librarian

Just as the social role of the library must inevitably change in an information-based society, the role of the librarian must change as well. Given the infinite complexity and the unlimited character of human information needs, I do not think it is likely that society's dependence on the skilled information professional will diminish.

Rather, I think it likely that that dependency will grow. As Stuart Brand points out in his thoughtful assessment of the significance of MIT's Media Lab, "New technologies create new freedoms and new dependencies." Brand warns, "The freedoms are more evident at first. The dependencies may never become evident, which makes them all the worse, because then it takes a crisis to discover them."[12]

I believe that the new technology is serving to empower both those who use libraries and those who staff libraries. I believe it is already altering the character of the reference process as well. For example, as telecommunication is substituted for face-to-face communication, librarians no longer have the ability to monitor the outcomes of the information-seeking process in conventional ways. What is potentially lost is what Shoshana Zuboff terms "personalism . . . a felt linkage between the knower and the known." The consequence for both information seeker and information mediator may be analogous to what Zuboff observes as a frequent characteristic of automated work environments, where digital symbols replace the concrete reality of the printed page: "feelings of loss of control, of vulnerability, and of frustration."[13] I recently had the opportunity to observe firsthand both the new dependency that computerization can create and the frustration that can accompany that dependency. In a large university library that has converted to an online public access catalog, the conversion has been accompanied by a change in staffing level at the public catalog information desk, where student assistants have replaced professional librarians. A student, trying to determine whether the library owned a book published some ten years ago, was told by the desk attendant that, because the system was down, there was no way to find out. That pronouncement, which elicited considerable frustration from the information seeker, was made directly in front of the card catalog, where consulting the cards in one tray would have provided the needed information.

This anecdote illustrates my thesis that information technology neither diminishes the importance of the reference librarian nor, in and of itself, improves the quality of service to the information seeker. There is, however, one significant benefit to library users that *can* be realized as a consequence of bibliographic technology. As Allen Veaner points out in a thoughtful appraisal of the changing role of the academic librarian, technology now makes it possible to delegate what he terms "production work. . .the burden of bibliographic housekeeping" to support staff. This in turn, Veaner suggests, should make it possible for technical services librarians to join public service librarians in "a united professional cadre capable of complementing faculty through several invaluable roles: research colleague, bibliographic expert, information system manager, and information system use instructor."[14]

Finally, it seems to me, the computerization of the bibliographic enterprise does potentially have the power to alter some of the implicit hierarchies that have characterized the functional division of labor in larger libraries for the last thirty years. If Harlan Cleveland is correct in his observation that "the aptitudes and attitudes of the generalist" will become the sine qua non of leadership in the information society, then the era of the dominance of the subject specialist bibliographer may be coming to an end.[15] It is not difficult to envision expert systems that could provide quite satisfactory access to the basic bibliographic structure of each of the principal scholarly disciplines.

As more and more of the production work of bibliographic organization can be delegated to support staff, more higher-level professional energy can be directed to improving and upgrading the quality of reference and information services. Just as technical services attracted more than a fair share of the most talented entry-level librarians in the 1960s and 1970s, so public services seem to be experiencing a resurgence in the 1980s, especially as a consequence of the revival of interest in bibliographic instruction. As the availability of more powerful technology puts greater resources at the command of the professional at the information desk, that individual may simultaneously have greater scope and greater freedom to exercise independent professional judgment in determining the extent of the institution's response to a given reference inquiry.

Conclusion

To summarize, technology is changing, and will continue to change, the character of reference and information service in libraries of all types and sizes. Whether those changes result in more access to more useful information for a larger portion of the library's actual or potential clientele will depend on our ability, as information professionals, to define and achieve the higher levels of service that are responsive to enhanced user expectations. As Milo Nelson pointed out in his final *Wilson Library Bulletin* editorial in January of this year: "What seems clear is that our salvation will not lie in databases or information systems any more than it was in books. Our future will reside in more perfectly understanding and serving our public. We don't need just more money and technology. We need more vision."[16]

Notes

1. Clement Bezold and Robert Olson, *The Information Millenium: Alternative Futures* (Washington, D.C.: Information Industry Association, 1986).

2. Ibid., 6-7.

3. Ibid., 1-5.

4. Ibid., 5.

5. American Library Association, Presidential Committee on Information Literacy, *Final Report,* January 1989, 1.

6. Ibid., 2.

7. Steven Muller, "Future Changes in Academic Programs and Structures," in *Universities, Information Technology, and Academic Libraries: The Next Twenty Years* (Los Angeles: University of California, Los Angeles, 1982), 124.

8. Presidential Committee on Information Literacy, 11.

9. W. F. Lancaster, "Future Librarianship: Preparing for an Unconventional Career," *Wilson Library Bulletin,* May 1983, 749-50.

10. Arthur D. Little, Inc., *The Los Angeles Public Library/In the Information Age* (Boston, November 1981), III-6.

11. Harvey Wheeler, *The Virtual Library: The Electronic Library Developing within the Traditional Library* (Los Angeles: Doheny Documents, University of Southern California, 1987), ii.

12. Stewart Brand, *The Media Lab: Inventing the Future at MIT* (New York: Penguin Books, 1988), 226-27.

13. Shoshana Zuboff, *In the Age of the Smart Machine* (New York: Basic Books, 1988), 61-63.

14. Allen Veaner, "1985 to 1995: The Next Decade in Academic Librarianship, Part 1," *College & Research Libraries,* May 1985, 216-17, 222.

15. Harlan Cleveland, *The Knowledge Executive: Leadership in an Information Society* (New York: Dutton, 1985), 4.

16. Milo Nelson, "Ten Years of Commotion and Distillation," *Wilson Library Bulletin,* January 1989, 4.

Part 2
Resource Sharing and Collection Development

ILL: The Backbone of Materials Sharing

DAVID H. BRUNELL
Executive Director
Bibliographic Center for Research
Denver, Colorado

Introduction: Changes and Trends in ILL

Interlibrary loan remains the backbone of materials sharing and the basis of most library resource sharing in this country, as it has been for at least the last fifty years. That is not to say, however, that interlibrary loan practices have not changed and changed dramatically in this country, particularly in the last decade.

While overall statistics on national interlibrary loan levels are difficult to gather and even more difficult to interpret, it is clear that the level of ILL activity has grown significantly from the level of twenty-five million requests that King research estimated in 1981.[1] In addition, if the recent trends in the BCR member states of Utah, Colorado, Kansas, Iowa, and Wyoming are any indication of national trends, then the growth rate for ILL has been significantly higher than the 9 percent annual increase that Boss and McQueen estimated in 1983.[2]

It is true that the accelerated growth of interlibrary loan in the Rocky Mountain and Plains region may have been influenced by the regional economic problems that have severely limited collection expansion in libraries of all types. At least in Colorado, it seems clear that the growth in ILL has been between 14 and 18 percent over the last few years.[3]

However, I suspect that the overwhelming adoption of OCLC by the larger libraries in the region, combined with the development of a number of effective local microcomputer-based ILL systems, the introduction of telefacsimile systems for document delivery, and a major use of a statewide CD ROM based locator system, have also significantly influenced the growth of ILL in the region. The plain fact is that these automated tools make interlibrary loan service considerably more efficient and reliable. The use of automated systems and their influence on ILL practice are what I would like to talk about today.

The Effect of New Technology on ILL

It seems clear that the widespread use of the OCLC system has had an enduring and significant effect on national ILL practice and patterns. Waldhart's article on the performance evaluation of interlibrary loan cites a dozen or more studies that show that the use of OCLC cuts turnaround time and increases the overall efficiency of ILL practices by simplifying bibliographic verification, communicating requests quickly, and keeping reliable ILL records and statistics.[4]

This increase in efficiency, tied to the use of the OCLC cataloging system, has created the most reliable and timely materials-locating tool that libraries in this country have ever had widely available. It is also clear that the use of OCLC has an additional impact by leveling the ILL load, making small libraries frequent lenders for the first time.[5]

Other computer-based ILL systems have been developed both in centralized bibliographic utilities, such as RLIN or WLN, and by commercial vendors (particularly those with shared circulation and online public access systems): A number of other ILL systems have been developed for use with microcomputer systems by local networks.[6] However, OCLC's system has been by far the most influential system because well over twenty-one hundred libraries in this country use the system regularly. In fiscal year 1988 3,781,000 ILL transactions were completed on the OCLC system; they are now occurring at the rate of about 75,000 requests per week.[7]

Many RLIN member libraries are also major users of the OCLC ILL system. As a matter of fact, two out of the three RLIN libraries in the BCR region make considerably greater use of the OCLC ILL system than they do of the RLIN ILL system.

It is interesting to note, however, that many of the benefits that accrue to OCLC users are also beginning to be seen by libraries that have implemented shared circulation and OPAC systems. An example of this can been seen in Colorado where the members of the CARL system experienced an increase in the use of ILL even before they developed an automated ILL system. Patrons using their shared online public access catalog were able to locate items easily in nearby libraries, and so began to request those items. Patrons were even more likely to simply go to the other library and check out the materials on their own, and the increase in cross-library use by patrons from other CARL members was even more marked.[8] This was possible because the online public access catalog is tied to a shared circulation system, letting patrons know whether or not a given item is checked out and simplifying bibliographic verification. All this has led the CARL libraries to begin development and testing of a patron initiated ILL system, which will not, in theory at least, require the intervention of ILL librarians to initiate requests.

CD ROM-based locating tools are also being widely used for the first time. At least ten major projects are being implemented across the country at this time, with another dozen or so in the planning stage. We have already seen the implementation of the Pennsylvania Access project, which has placed several hundred CD ROM systems in schools and public libraries. The CD ROM-based Iowa locator system has recently begun another phase, which has added over a quarter of a million additional holdings to the database and extended the system to almost a hundred small public libraries.[9]

The reduction in the cost of telefacsimile has also begun to have a significant impact on ILL recently. While the computer-based systems I have talked about so far affect both the creation and the transmittal of the request, FAX machines have the potential of revolutionizing the delivery of the requested material. It is estimated that one-third to one-half of the current ILL load consists of requests for serial articles, and the newest generation of FAX machines have the required resolution and speed to transmit almost all of this load efficiently.

ILL at the End of the Twentieth Century

The advances in technology have certainly changed interlibrary loan practice in this country, particularly over the last ten years. In most libraries the majority of ILL transactions are now received and transmitted via a computerized system. In many cases the ILL department has access to several computerized systems. Major resource libraries, such as the University of Colorado at Boulder, may regularly use half a dozen different systems as they send requests on OCLC, the National Library of Medicine (NLM) network, the regional CARL system, and several local systems. In addition, they have access to several CD ROM-based systems.

While this use of advanced technology has improved their fill rate, decreased turnaround time for transactions, and arguably made ILL more efficient, we should also note that it has made ILL services more complex and considerably more expensive than in the past.10 Richard De Gennaro has cited this as an example of Butler's Law: "Libraries cannot tolerate marked increases in the 'success level' of their operation."11 Butler's Law remains true, of course, only as long as library administrators fail to convince funding agencies that such library services are cost-effective.

In fact, the increase in direct expense and the need to recoup this expense have led to the widespread practice of charging for ILL services by all types of libraries. While many states have developed reimbursement schemes for net lenders, these schemes seldom pay anywhere near the real cost incurred. This, in turn, has lead some public librarians to question the whole resource-sharing enterprise.12 Fortunately, most of the profession seems to have retained a commitment to modern ILL services and the networking that makes them possible.

As a matter of fact, I would suggest that the general acceptance of ILL costs and practices has led us to ignore some possible changes in ILL practice that could make ILL services more cost-effective. A recent article by Bell and Speer questioning the need for bibliographic verification of ILL requests is an interesting exception to this.13 This article suggests that most verification, although required by the ALA model ILL code, is unnecessary. Certainly, to the extent that library customers garner ILL requests from online databases, verification may be automatic. It would follow, then, that patron-generated ILL systems like the one being developed by the CARL libraries may be both possible and successful.

We have not moved from the effort to offer efficient document delivery to the idea of offering information delivery services, perhaps because of the reluctance of library users to accept information rather than documents. You may recall Dr. McCaleb's comments in this context. Note that we have not even reached the "black hole between data and knowledge" that Dr. Penniman spoke of in his keynote address. It is possible to conceive of the dovetailing of patron-initiated ILL and expert systems that would result, not in the delivery of documents or even data, but in the presentation of knowledge that is data arranged coherently, which would actually answer the questions posed by library users without the intervention of librarians.

Notes

1. King Research, *Libraries, Publishing and Photocopying: Final Report of Surveys Conducted for the United States Copyright Office* (Rockville, Md.: King Research, 1982).

2. Richard Boss and Judy McQueen, *Document Delivery in the United States: A Report to the Council on Library Resources* (Washington, D.C.: CLR, 1983), 7.

3. *Statistics and Input-Output Measures for Colorado Public Libraries* (Denver: Colorado State Library, 1988).

4. Thomas J. Waldhart, "Performance Evaluation of Interlibrary Loan in the United States: A Review of Research," *LISR* 7 (1985): 318-19. See also Peter Abbott and Rosemary Kavanagh, "Electronic Resource Sharing

Changes Interloan Patterns," *Library Journal* 111, no. 16 (1 October 1986): 56-58.

5. This was predicted by Fred Kilgour a decade ago and appears to have been a national trend. See Frederick G. Kilgour, "Interlibrary Loans On-line," *Library Journal* 104, no. 4 (1 March 1979): 460-63.

6. Waldart, "Performance Evaluation," 327. See also Ed Volz, "A Survey of Automated Interlibrary Loan in Colorado," *Colorado Libraries* 13, no. 4 (December 1987): 11-12.

7. *OCLC Annual Report, 1987/88: Furthering Access to the World's Information* (Dublin, Ohio: OCLC, 1988), 1.

8. Ward Shaw, "Local Networking–Colorado Alliance of Research Libraries," *Colorado Libraries* 13, no. 4 (December 1987): 8.

9. Doris M. Epler and Richard E. Cassel, "Access Pennsylvania: A CD-ROM Database Project," *Library Hi Tech* 5, no. 19 (1987): 81-92. See also "New Iowa Locator Released to 70 Sites," *Footnotes* 13, no. 5 (March 1989): 6.

10. Note that we are referring to the direct cost of using such tools and systems. To the extent that use reduces staff time, we can actually document an overall reduction in the cost of ILL service. However, as we all know, a librarian's time is free.

11. Richard De Gennaro, *Library Technology and Information Marketplace: Selected Papers* (Boston: G. K. Hall, 1987), 275-76.

12. An example of this viewpoint can be found in Thomas Ballard, *The Failure of Resource Sharing in Public Libraries and Alternative Strategies for Service* (Chicago: American Library Association, 1986).

13. Jo Ann Bell and Susan Speer, "Bibliographic Verification for Interlibrary Loan: Is it Necessary?" *College and Research Libraries* (November 1988): 494-500. Other studies have found significant problems with the patrons' ability to recognize material availability on online public access catalogs and circulation systems. See, for instance, Anne C. Ciliberti, Mary F. Casserly, Judith L. Hegg, and Eugene S. Mitchell, "Material Availability: A Study of Academic Library Performance,"*College and Research Libraries,* November 1987, 513-27.

Collection Development and the Influence of Resource Sharing

ANTHONY W. FERGUSON
Resources Library Director
Butler Library
Columbia University
New York, New York

Historical Background: 1876–1976

From early times libraries have sought to take advantage of the resources held in other collections. For example, in the early thirteenth century a register of manuscripts held in 138 different monasteries in England and Scotland was developed. Indeed, in a guide to building libraries published in 1627, the advice was given that one can "please a friend, when one cannot provide him the book he requires, by directing him to the place where he may find a copy."[1] We have not changed much in the ensuing years; we still seek to supplement our own institutions' collections and to please our users by providing them with information about the holdings of other libraries.

While my purpose is not to provide a detailed history of resource sharing and its influence or lack of influence upon collection development, I would like to begin by describing the major events that have shaped the environment in which our current resource-sharing efforts take place:

1876	A group of New York libraries began to develop standards for the exchange of cataloging records. Over time these exchanged cards were filed and became union catalogs.
1897	NYPL and Columbia drafted a cooperative collection development plan.
1898	The University of California announced that it would share with any other library willing to share.
1899	Princeton's librarian proposed that "a lending library for libraries" be established.

Before the turn of the century we already had cooperative cataloging, interlibrary loan (ILL), cooperative collection development, and the Center for Research Libraries' concept already in place. We have not really departed from these four basic resource-sharing concepts in this century. The technologies we have employed to accomplish these functions have changed a great deal:

1900	The National Union Catalog was established, and a year later the Library of Congress began selling cards. Over the next three decades, many other major libraries followed suit, with the purchasers copying the cataloging and using it for union catalogs.
1913-14	Northwestern University's librarian representing Harvard, Brown, the John Crerar Library and the American Antiquarian Society, went on a buying trip to eleven Latin American countries.
1927	The *Union List of Serials* was published.
1930s	A variety of regional groupings of libraries (e.g., Duke and North Carolina, Claremont Colleges) agree to cooperatively acquire, process and lend their holdings.
1932	LC's cooperative cataloging program began, and within ten years four hundred libraries were participants.

1942	A cooperative storage facility for a number of Boston area libraries was developed.
1946	The LC began a project that in three years distributed over a million volumes published in Europe during World War II to 113 American libraries.
1948	The Universal Serial and Book Exchange, Inc., was established. The Farmington plan began operation. This was the most ambitious cooperative collection development program, which distributed tens of thousands of books annually to fifty to sixty of America's research libraries.
1951	The precursor to the Center for Research Libraries was established.
1956	Managed by the Association for Research Libraries, the Foreign Newspaper Microfilm, was initiated.
1959	The Latin American Cooperative Acquisitions Program began and sold books to about forty research libraries.
1961	The PL 480 program began.
1967	The Ohio College Library Center was incorporated.
1973	The Research Libraries Group was established.

Everything I have listed so far is discussed in David Weber's very readable "A Century of Cooperative Programs among Academic Libraries," published in the May 1976 issue of *College and Research Libraries*.[2] Even those most distrustful of interlibrary cooperation, reading this account, will be impressed with the increase in use of the resource-sharing tools in order to meet the needs of library users.

At the same time, it is interesting to ask the question, What impact have these cooperative endeavors had upon the collection development activities of America's research libraries during the same period of time? The overall answer to this question is not much. Some might suppose that this is because, unlike now, libraries in those years were not faced with the "too many books, too little money" problem. Actually this wasn't the case. It has been estimated that American university libraries accelerated their average annual acquisitions rate between 1875 and 1920 from 1,168 volumes to 15,707 volumes. Still, there were some ten million books and seventy thousand journals out there to be pursued if American university libraries were to catch up with their European counterparts.[3] America's libraries were very conscious of the impossible task facing them. In a 1912 survey of America's major university library holdings on European history, of the 2,197 titles included in the assessment Harvard had only 1,600, which was more than all the other libraries had put together.[4]

This could have been a watershed period. America's political and cultural leaders could have come together and rationally decided that its universities could never build the needed library resources. An enforced centralized or decentralized cooperative collection development system could have been instituted. But in the fiercely independent America of the early 1900s, that was impossible. Instead, scholars in individual departments who needed the raw material for their own and their students' research pursued the funds to buy as many books and journals as possible. Not only was cooperation *not* employed among university libraries, but it was seldom found within large institutions either. Large universities were highly decentralized, with little coordination among departmental libraries. This further discouraged attempts to coordinate collection development. While some may view all of this competition negatively as a waste of resources it also facilitated the building of library collections on a scale unlike anything earlier in history.[5]

World War I and the depression had some impact on collection building, but it was World War II that brought a temporary end to all of this growth and the easy importation of the world's scholarship. The major collections had to work with each other and with the Library of Congress to make up for lack of access to their commercial vendors. This enforced cooperation carried on after the war under the Farmington plan, but political stability reestablished good relationships with European vendors; the rapid expansion of funds under the Higher Education Act of 1965 returned libraries to their national diet of competition. The actors by this time had changed, but the script remained the same. Librarians, instead of the faculty, were now in charge of what was purchased but they were still trying to meet the voracious needs of their users. This was further fueled by Sputnik, which rapidly increased the size and intensity of America's educational enterprise and rekindled the publishing industry.[6] The librarians of the 1970s found themselves in the same position as those running libraries a century earlier, with one exception: They now had increased needs to go along with their too many books, and too few dollars.

Post-1976 Developments

While resource sharing might have had little impact on the daily practice of collection developers in the past, clearly there are signs that this is changing. In 1983 Joe A. Hewitt and John S. Shipman of the University of North Carolina surveyed libraries belonging to the Association for Research Libraries about their participation in cooperative collection development activities. These libraries mentioned seventy programs in which they were or had been members. It is evident that the number of such programs is on the increase.[7]

Dates	*Number of Programs Begun*
1860s	1
1930	3
1950s	4
1960s	7
1970-74	2
1975-79	30
1980-83	23

Four other findings by Hewitt and Shipman about cooperative efforts among these ARL libraries also attest to the increased role that resource sharing is playing in our lives:

a. Most (80 percent) were participating in or planning to take part in such activities.

b. Most of these activities developed parallel to the advent of online bibliographic networks since the mid-1970s.

c. Reasons for nonparticipation relate more to the lack of suitable partners, organizations, technologies, or procedures rather than resistance to the concept of cooperation.

d. Most programs entailed the extension of special borrowing privileges.

When asked why they were involved in these programs, librarians indicated they wanted to:

a. Expand the range of research materials available to the community involved in the program.

b. Reduce duplication of expensive research materials.

c. Generally "coordinate" development of collections and acquisitions of materials.

d. Jointly acquire materials.

In a 1985 RLG study of selection decisions made by German and geology materials selectors, it was discovered that for research (as opposed to curricular support) materials, German materials selectors were willing to change 40 percent of their selection decisions and geology selectors 50 percent of their selection decisions and rely upon other libraries if they knew in advance it was possible.[8] The same study indicated, however, that these same selectors spent "very little expressly to satisfy consortial or other contractual obligations."[9] Clearly, we are closer to working in a cooperative mode than ever before. Librarians are thinking cooperatively. We have yet to find ways of going beyond single ILL transactions in order to put our thoughts into action.

Roadblocks to Resource Sharing

If librarians at least on the surface seem willing to rely upon others – and indeed they appear to be involved in an increasing array of activities – why is it that cooperative collection development has yet to become an everyday means of supplying a large part of our users' needs? The literature, buffered by my own experience, suggests that the expansion of coordinated collection development beyond its existing boundaries is retarded because of three factors.[10]

We lack:

a. Sufficient information about the strengths and weaknesses of our own and others' collections. We are uncertain of what we can bring to the cooperative effort, and we are distrustful that contents of other collections are sufficient.

b. Sufficient information about the demands of our own patrons and of others who might rely upon our resources.

We fear:

a. Loss of competitiveness with peers with whom we might cooperate.

b. Loss of autonomy of action.

c. Inadequate future resources to meet commitments.

d. Other participants not meeting their obligations.

e. Resource sharing being viewed by users as a failure to support their research and curricular needs.

We face certain inherent difficulties:

a. Time-consuming processes associated with document delivery, irrespective of the amount of electronic technology employed, make access an inadequate alternative to ownership.

b. Distances between user and the source of the information make borrowing difficult.

c. To rely upon others for current imprints requires immediate acquisitions and in-process information.

d. Users lack the ability to browse in order to serendipitously discover useful materials.

Can we overcome these inadequacies, fears, and inherent roadblocks? I believe we already have or are in the process of making great strides in overcoming the lack of information about the strengths and weaknesses of our collections, other collections, and our users' needs.

Overcoming What We Lack

The RLG Conspectus now in its many transformations is becoming an accepted part of our lives; for example, National Collections Inventory Project and Pacific Northwest Inventory. Through it, we have a common way of describing our collections to each other. As it becomes the de facto policy statement for most libraries, we will learn a great deal about our own collections and our users' needs.[11] As more and more libraries employ the Conspectus methodology, the lack of information about our own capacities, needs, and the capacities of other libraries to meet our less critical needs will fade.

Overcoming What We Fear

The conspectus, however, attacks only the first of these roadblocks to cooperative collection development. Our fears about the consequences of relying upon others and being relied upon are real and need to be addressed. Recently a concept has been evolving in the Research Libraries Group that may help overcome these fears. It is called the Cooperative Collecting Responsibility (CCR). Early on in RLG, a less comprehensive resource sharing concept was developed, called the Primary Collecting Responsibility (PCR). It was designed to ensure that unique, narrow collecting areas discovered through the conspectus process would continue to be collected.

Usually, this meant asking the one library interested in the topic (e.g., Czechoslovakian heraldry) to continue to collect and stop only after petitioning the other member libraries for permission. Since no one else cared, a library was safe in taking on such a responsibility. Any attempt, however, to use this same PCR concept to ensure coverage of an area important to several members of the consortium ended in failure because of the fear factor. Libraries could not do anything that would render their users less competitive or cause them to lose their ability to change with developments on their own campuses. Nor could they rely upon such guarantees from others. Above all they had to avoid the appearance of sacrificing local in favor of national needs.[12]

The Cooperative Collecting Responsibility, on the other hand, differs from a PCR. Instead of assigning one library the responsibility for collecting in a major area of interest (e.g., German literature), several libraries already collecting at the research level are given the assignment to work together. An earlier variation of this concept was initiated by RLG's East Asian Collections. In that case they divided up the provinces and metropolitan areas of China to ensure that beyond the basic nationally distributed materials that all of their libraries would require, the production of local and regional presses will be better represented in American libraries than would otherwise be possible. In both of these cases libraries are not cutting back in areas critical to user needs; rather, they are taking advantage of each other's strengths. To do this effectively, however, the number of participants involved and the existing levels of their collecting strength must be fairly high. Collective weaknesses do not constitute strength. Also, just a few large libraries cannot divide up all the responsibilities and base these decisions upon preexisting self-interests.[13]

Another development among RLG libraries relates to a number of long-term serials projects. Once again the emphasis is upon shared responsibilities. Currently, business, chemistry, and mathematics groups are experimenting with a variety of techniques of working together. For the sake of this presentation, a few words about how the mathematics group is proceeding will be illustrative. This group of materials selectors, using telephone conference calls and electronic mail, have developed and shared with each other a fairly exhaustive list of serials important to the field. The list, based upon frequency of subscriptions, has been divided into core and noncore divisions. Each library, according to its means, commits to subscribe to a portion of the core and a portion of the lesser held titles. Several libraries commit to core titles, while obscure titles already held by a single library are assigned to that library. This is a combination of CCR and PCR methodologies. By working together, these libraries can cover the list completely. Individually, no single library could possibly subscribe to all of these materials on behalf of their users. You'll note that in each of these RLG initiatives we are bringing bibliographers/materials selectors together–through piggybacking at ALA meetings, via e-mail, or on teleconference calls. In this way they are getting to know each other in the same way that selectors in a single library begin to build mutual trust and confidence. I project that, if this continues, we will approach making the national collection concept a reality. RLG now has a number of bibliographer groups, for example, German, English literature, social sciences, and documents. On a national scale this is a totally new development.

Overcoming Inherent Difficulties

My own feeling is that the cluster of inherent difficulties listed above that oppose resource sharing have prevented and will continue over the next five to ten years to prevent resource sharing from becoming a truly acceptable alternative to ownership of the materials themselves. All three problems relate to time–the time it takes:

a. For users to determine and communicate their needs that cannot be filled locally.

b. For the home library to identify who has the needed item.

c. For the home library to communicate the need.

d. For the lending library to respond to the user so that the search will not go on.

e. For the lending library to locate and pick up the item.

f. For the item to be shipped.

g. For the home library to communicate to the user that the item is available for pickup.

h. For the user to go back to the library and retrieve the item.

Using modern electronic technology, the time it takes to borrow resources from other libraries has been cut in some of the areas listed above:

a. For books already cataloged, shared bibliographic databases have greatly improved the following processes: identification, communication of need, and communication of whether the item can be lent. Two different approaches are being used with great effectiveness. In systems such as that used in Illinois, users share a common circulation system with which they themselves can quickly identify the item and its location. In some libraries, they can even initiate the loan themselves.[13] Among RLG and OCLC libraries, the required and already cataloged item can also be readily identified and information about it communicated to and from the lending institution through an ILL office that must be found and worked with. ILL use in Illinois has skyrocketed, but electronically enhanced but traditional ILL among bibliographic utility clients is still very limited compared to circulation of a library's own books.

b. The actual shipping of materials has been enhanced within regional cooperatives through the use of courier services. On the national scene UPS delivery, while more costly, is a great improvement. Soon faxing material among libraries will be as common as using the mail service.

We are still stymied by a number of very tough problems. First is the simple human problem of sending someone to the stacks to retrieve or track down the needed item, carry it to the ILL office for processing, pack it, and mailing it. A few years ago Malcolm Smith from the British Lending Library analyzed the ILL function in RLG libraries. He concluded that this area of handling was the problem, not the lack of sufficient electronic technology.[14]

Second is the lack of shared order files, access to information about newly acquired books, and backlogged materials awaiting cataloging data. In the early years of RLG it seemed we would share a common order file. With the development of integrated in-house library systems, any hope that research libraries had of sharing this kind of information via the bibliographic utilities is rapidly crumbling. True, the utilities have sped the processing of most materials–typically American or British imprints–but the very types of material needing the cooperative collection development solution languish in backlogs, out of electronic or human sight. While there has been some talk of the Linked Systems Project solving this dilemma, it is doubtful that this will be an economically feasible solution in the next five or more years. Work is also proceeding on the development of CD ROM databases of the holdings of library consortiums, which may be able to substitute for the lack of this type of information on our bibliographic utilities.[15]

Third, at least at the institutions where I've worked, we've done little to speed up the process of notifying the user that their request has been received. We've used sophisticated electronic technology to identify and request materials. Then they are unpacked in the batch mode and matched to the user, and a postcard is sent via campus mail. One to ten weeks after the time they first decided they wanted to look at the item they receive a postcard. Our part-time researchers then have to find time to go back to our interlibrary loan offices during the correct hours and retrieve books (which they wish they could have browsed on our shelves).

Despite all of these problems, we still borrow because the alternative for our users is much worse. All of these three factors are soluble. My own view is that collection development librarians need to recognize that ILL is not just a public service function and that we will have to support the reallocation of staff resources to ILL. Likewise, we must work with our technical services counterparts to ensure that there are ways to identify what is on order or in process at the libraries upon which we depend.

Conclusion

The effect of resource sharing on collection development among American libraries has increased enormously since the first cards about holdings were exchanged in the late 1800s. Virtually all libraries are involved in resource sharing,and only a few among us doubt its usefulness. We have developed ways of assessing our own capabilities and needs and communicating with each other about the strengths and weaknesses of our library collections. We are evolving ways of sharing with other libraries the responsibility of developing collections and moving away from simplistic notions of assigning German literature to one library and French to another. We have improved our methods of electronically communicating title-specific requirements and transferring the information or item between institutions.

We remain with a number of very difficult problems. We lack the ability to cost effectively share information about on-order or uncataloged materials. The cumulative effect of all the processes involved in an interlibrary loan transaction still render resource-sharing schemes an unacceptable alternative to ownership. We have made real progress, but our users are not yet willing to return to the inconvenience of even the closed-stack concept, let alone waiting the two to ten weeks that are so common between when they drop off their requests and pick up the wanted item.[16]

Notes

1. Joe W. Kraus, "Prologue to Library Cooperation," *Library Trends*, October 1975, 169.

2. David C. Weber, "A Century of Cooperative Programs among Academic Libraries," *College and Research Libraries*, May 1976, 205-10.

3. Hendrik Edelman and G. Marvin Tatum, Jr., "The Development of Collections in American University Libraries," *College and University Libraries*, May 1976, 225.

4. Ibid.

5. Ibid.

6. Ibid.

7. Joe A. Hewitt and John S. Shipman, "Cooperative Collection Development among Research Libraries in the Age of Networking: Report of a Survey of ARL Libraries," *Advances in Library Automation and Networking* 1 (1987): 197-203.

8. Jim Coleman, "Preliminary Report on the Conoco Study in German Literature and Geology" (Memorandum addressed to Steering Committee of the RLG Collection Management and Development Committee and Public Services Committee, 26 June 1986), 1.

9. Ibid., 2.

10. The literature on the inadequacies of interlibrary loan is voluminous. The following sources are not particularly against resource sharing, but each presents its failings (particular pages indicated). Thomas H. Ballard, "Dogma Clouds the Facts," *American Libraries* 16 (April 1985): 257-59; Scott Bennett, "Current Initiatives and Issues in Collection Development," *Journal of Academic Librarianship* 10 (November 1984): 260; Ralph Blasingame, "The Great Library in the Sky Prototype," *Library Journal* 97 (15 May 1972): 1771; Michael J. Carmel, "Library Resource Sharing in the National Health Service: Benefits and Limitations," *Interlending and Document Supply* 16 (1988): 14; Richard M. Dougherty, "The Paradoxes of Library Cooperation," *Library Journal* 97 (15 May 1972): 1768; Ward Shaw, "Cooperative Academic Library Networks: The CARL Experience," in "The First Annual I. I. Littleton Seminar," ed. Jinnie Y. Davis and Margaret Ann Link, *The Southeastern Librarian*, Summer 1988, 53-54; Thomas T. Galvin, "Not in Our Stars But in Ourselves," *Library Journal* 97 (15 May 1972): 1772; George F. Heise, "Barriers to Cooperative Computerized Circulation Systems in Public Libraries," *Resource Sharing and Information Networks* 3 (Fall 1985/Winter 1985-86): 85-88; James O. Lehman, "Cooperation among Small Academic Libraries," *College and Research Libraries* 30 (November 1969): 496; Robert F. Munn, "Collection Development vs. Resource Sharing: The Dilemma of the Middle-Level Institutions," *Journal of Academic Librarianship* 12 (July 1986): 166-67; Rodrick G. Swartz, "The Need for Cooperation among Libraries in the United States," *Library Trends* 24 (October 1975): 219.

11. Anthony W. Ferguson, Joan Grant, and Joel S. Rutstein, "The RLG Conspectus: Its Uses and Benefits," *College and Research Libraries* 49 (May 1988): 197-206.

12. Anthony W. Ferguson, "Expanding the PCR: Discussion Piece" (White paper prepared for RLG Collection Management and Development Committee Meeting, 12 September 1988, at Brown University).

13. Bernard G. Sloan, "Resource Sharing among Academic Libraries: The LCS Experience," *Journal of Academic Librarianship* 12 (March 1986): 26-29.

14. Malcolm D. Smith, "A Project to Improve Interlibrary Loans within the Research Libraries Group, Executive Summary" (Consultant's Report, 1984).

15. Norman A. Stevens, "Library Networks and Resource Sharing in the United States: An Historical and Philosophical Overview," *Journal of the American Society for Information Science* 31 (November 1980): 408.

16. Ballard, "Dogma Clouds the Facts," 257.

Part 3
Serving Our Varied Clientele

Slaying Dragons: Overcoming Obstacles to Excellence in Youth Services

MARY R. SOMERVILLE
Children's Coordinator
Broward County Library
Ft. Lauderdale, Florida

In the PBS series "The Power of Myth," Joseph Campbell said that each of us creates our own myth and lives by it. As librarians, especially in youth services, we may feel that there's nothing Greek, Roman, or even Grimm in our daily challenges: facing conflicts over budgets, lacking staff to serve increasing hordes of young patrons, deflecting patronizing remarks about our work. Caught up in everyday trivia, we fail to see that when we justify budgets, keep on keeping on, and against all odds provide outstanding services and programs, we are slaying dragons.

The first dragon we have to combat is cynicism – our own and that of others. This cynicism is more insidious by virtue of being an unspoken assumption. It goes like this: "According to census statistics, ours is a graying population, with fewer youth despite the current baby boom. Since the library serves the 'total population' and since that population is aging, we need to downplay youth services." Sound like a myth? It was a reality I faced in Louisville, Kentucky, ten years ago, when an ALA-hired group of researchers marched in and announced that conclusion before the first survey was fired. Had it not been for then-director Ronald Kozlowski (now at Cuyahoga County Library) and visiting consultant William Summers (now ALA president and dean of the library school at Florida State University), support for Louisville's youth services might have gone down the tubes. As an interesting footnote, during those ten years, Summer Reading participation and children's circulation skyrocketed, while a flagging blue collar economy and general lack of public tax support for adult services have reordered Louisville's priorities. According to Director William Ptacek, the Louisville Free Public Library hopes to "build a library community for the long-term through kids." Evidence of the new emphasis is the countywide library card campaign, last year reaching ninty thousand public school students and this year extending to forty thousand parochial school children and young adults (YAs).

Why the Researchers Were Wrong

What happened? Why were the researchers so offbase? They assumed that the public library really does reach the total population, rather than a sharply focused market. Theatre owners understand market analysis; Hollywood does, as it serves up countless adolescent movies for predominantly young adult audiences. Businesses of all types, including Toys Are Us, understand that one's clientele is not the total population, as library directors love to say. The truth is, we serve women and youth first. If your computer registers patrons by sex and birth date, you can test my hypothesis, or you can survey your patrons by age and sex, comparing their numbers in the census with numbers related to library usage, or you can look out on the floor on a typical morning, afternoon, and evening.

Broward County Library is an interesting case in point. We might call it the "magic library system" because it grew up almost overnight, shaped by the considerable political and visionary skills of Director Cecil Beach. A few small municipal libraries were assimilated gradually into what is now a still-growing system of twenty four libraries with 550 employees. The award-winning main library is only five years old. The director states, "When we came to Broward County, children's work had never been emphasized, probably because the earliest Fort Lauderdale settlement was by retirees." Apathy toward youth services was reflected in the fact that there were no professional children's (or young adult) librarians in the first libraries. Children's collections were not well developed. As we put the system together and took note of where we were, it became apparent that we needed to do something about youth services. Demographic studies showed that Broward County's newest spurt of growth was among children and young adults, owing to the influx of high-tech industries that attract young families. Therefore, we decided to slay the dragon of having no professional youth librarians and to bring the level of children's and young adult work up to par with other areas of the library. While our youth usage figures here don't exactly match Louisville's yet, there's room for expansion and tremendous demand for service. We are in the process of establishing young adult services and enhancing children's services.

Why Libraries Skimp on Children and Young Adults

In talking with children's and young adult librarians nationally, as I did in writing this article, I found that the problem is not really a dearth of child and young adult users. The problem is justifying that need and receiving concrete support, dollar for dollar. There's often a yawning gap between usage and dollars allocated, partly because two other dragons rear their heads: (1) the assumption that youth have no political clout, and (2) the conclusion that because children and young adults are powerless, they will accept mediocrity. Neither assumption is true.

Let's take the first assumption, the perceived lack of political clout. As in the Louisville example, youth services can be used to promote PR and community support. People also point to Atlanta's successful bond issue of a few years ago, in which posters of sad-eyed children won the day. A $27 million bond issue just passed in Richland County, South Carolina, features this campaign slogan: "Don't Close the Book on our Children's Future." Likewise, Bush's campaign videos showed him swinging his grandchild in the air. All politicians love to be photographed kissing babies. Where YAs may not be so kissable, they can still rally support. Christy Tyson, formerly of Spokane, Washington, now of Alabama Public Library Service, likes to tell the story of how members of the library's YA advisory group rallied grassroots political support for YA services while she was on vacation. Several years back, in assembling a never-published article on just this topic (it is resting comfortably in the archives of one of your favorite library magazines), I asked library directors Regina Minudri, Ronald Kozlowski, Sara Long, Agnes Griffin, and others to respond. They all said the same thing, or to quote Regina: "Library service to youth is as American as mom and apple pie."

Yet another dragon limiting youth services' budgets is the unspoken assumption that children and young adults are not quite bright; using this line of reasoning, we think we can give youth token, mediocre service, and they won't even notice. No assumption could be more in error. Anyone who has ever addressed college students, as I have, faced a group of two-year-olds in story hour, or visited a classroom of adolescents to deliver a booktalk will tell you that far greater preparation, creativity, imagination, and effort must go into delivery of the story hour or booktalk. Children and young adults are tough audiences, knowing and demanding the best, whether in programs, collections, or services. A child may not immediately react to less than equal service, but that child will not forget. Just ask Freud. Still, the mediocrity myth prevails, used as justification for skimpy youth services' budgets, staffing, and pay scales.

How We Extend Service to Children and Young Adults

How do we turn the situation around, rallying support for excellence in youth services? First, we need to assemble relevant data. This is often more easily said than done. Paperbacks, key to children's and YA circulation, are not always counted by automated systems, and hand-kept figures aren't convincing at budget time. Second, whereas children's hardback circulation figures may be more readily available, YA figures are largely elusive. Most libraries have, at best, small browser collections of YA hardbacks, which may or may not possess the separate classification required to produce a valid circulation count. In terms of circulation, young adult usage becomes a matter of myth or conjecture. The fact that many libraries have integrated children's and adult nonfiction can be used as a weapon against youth collection building. People say, "Adults are checking out children's books," never the reverse, nor do they realize that many day care, elementary, and high school teachers are checking out materials to share with a wider youth audience.

Then there's the matter of registration. Unless your automated system registers patrons by birth date, you'll find it difficult to count total youth registrations. The eternal debate over the exact age group constituting "young adult" enters in here, further complicating things. Each library needs to make that determination, then find a way–perhaps a survey–to count the percentage of child and young adult registrations.

Once those figures are available, we need to add reference statistics. Some libraries tally the number of reference questions asked by students, but few libraries count percentages of questions asked by elementary, middle school, and high school students, nor do they make a concerted effort to coordinate such student demands with staffing or collection development.

Although there are government documents and fine arts librarians, very few staff members are actually designated school assignment librarians. In most branch and main libraries, reference librarians are considered part of adult services; thus, they rarely focus on school assignments and may even consider student questions an intrusion on time spent serving "serious" adult concerns. Again, libraries need to determine, by survey or by tally, what percentage of questions answered are for different student categories. If that percentage is substantial, a designated number of appropriate reference librarians needs to concentrate on serving student interests and coordinating efforts with schools in terms of homework assignments. While reference librarians may be generalists, they still have some specialized subject assignments. Courteous and committed service to students needs to be included in the list of basic service specialties.

Nationally, the Association for Library Service to Children (ALSC) and the Public Library Association (PLA) have appointed a joint task force to study the application of output measures to children's services. The recently completed (May 1989) symposium at the University of Wisconsin also focused on the need for concrete evaluation of youth services. The ALA joint task force was created because output measures did not lend themselves to a survey of children, who cannot understand and interpret complex written instructions. Likewise, we need a firmer grasp of YA output measures. In short, we need to know the percentage of registration, circulation, and reference use attributable to children and young adults.

One step in the right direction is a set of twin surveys being conducted by the U.S. Department of Education. Already completed is the young adult portion (fall 1987). Results show that "one out of every four public library patrons in 1986-87 was a young adult (between the ages of 12 and 18)."[1] A future survey of children will further spotlight youth usage figures. It is entirely within the realm of possibility that, taken together, the two surveys will support a youth usage pattern of 50 percent.

How We Can Handle the Library Budget

Once we have assembled concrete figures, both locally and nationally, we can seek to conquer the greatest dragon of them all: the library budget. More often than not, youth services receives crumbs rather than a proportionate share of the loaf. Let's start with library materials monies, which are usually allocated by what we might call the grab-bag approach, in which heads of branches and departments meet to plead for departmental needs. In political contests like this, youth librarians are especially vulnerable. For one thing, decisions rarely rest on solid figures. For another, youth librarians are not in the power position. As middle managers, they are often outnumbered by representatives from adult services; in branches, the branch head, not the children's librarian, calls the shots. Without a more equal system based on solid data and equal representation, youth services is bound to lose out.

Before distributing the materials budget, several factors need to be considered.

First, *for circulating materials* (especially applicable to children's materials, for reasons stated above):

- The age of materials circulated by children's and YA classifications, including paperbacks.

- The average cost of an adult versus a children's book, including higher discounts given adult materials (often 25 percent for children's books; 40 percent or more for adult books).

- The condition of materials on the shelf.

Children's materials get rougher use by small children. With PLB bindings getting worse and worse, heavily used picture books fall apart promptly. Libraries need to either allocate more monies to bind these materials or shell out monies for replacement/duplicate copies, increasing the amount given to picture books, for example, because of wear and tear and binding factors.

> *Final Jeopardy Question:* How much money is taken off the top for rental or purchase of adult best-sellers before dividing the budget into adult, children's, and YA categories? Rental of best-sellers needs to be considered part of the adult overall figure.

Second, *for reference* materials (especially appropriate for middle and high school students):

- Percentage of questions by students ages 18 and under.

- Types of questions. A case in point is that libraries are deluged with requests for help by students in science fair projects; adult librarians don't always consider such questions serious, nor do they allocate monies to supply the demand. Here in Broward County, Main Library business, science, and technology head Jean Anderson not only saw the need but initiated a grant request to support that need; she remembered her own frustration in trying to locate materials for her son, who became a National Merit Scholar.

- Online and CD ROM sources. These are usually considered primarily for adults, whereas children and YAs are far more conversant with new technology and are therefore more likely to use it.

> *Final Jeopardy Question:* Given the percentage of youth questions, what percentage of monies for reference materials, usually taken off the top for book, CD ROM, and online resources, is being dedicated to answer homework and other youth reference questions?

Then we come to budgets for programs. Here we *do* have concrete figures. However, those figures may or may not matter, depending on the scheme of things. Huge numbers of children attend programs; however, I know of at least one situation in which adult programs received twice the money for one-tenth the audience, owing to the mediocrity-for-youth myth.

Also, budgets for basics such as staffing, space, furniture, and equipment need to be examined and made relative to actual patron use. Why does a branch whose primary clientele is children still give the lion's share of space and furniture to adults? Because adults are larger? Because we keep hoping they'll predominate? If, as we anticipate, as much as half library usage is by youth, why do librarians serving them get paid so much less? Why are they relegated to beginning positions? Why is there no backup provided for their story hours and reference desks while the adult reference desk is considered primary?

There is a recurring pattern of patronizing remarks and responses toward youth services. How often has someone said to me, "I started out as a children's librarian," to which I am learning to reply, "I started out as a university teacher but found the 'publish-or-perish' mode intellectually and emotionally stultifying. That's why I got into youth services." ALA President Bill Summers announced that one of his goals is to build pride in library work. Such a campaign is desperately needed among youth librarians, and we require help and concrete support from administrators. When we deliver champagne service on beer budgets, we need bubbles in the form of accolades, real dollars, career ladders, and input into decision making. The bottom line is this: equal services with budgets, staffing, and pay allocated according to concrete usage patterns.

What Youth Librarians Can Accomplish

It's important to remember that there's strength in numbers. Youth librarians need to network nationally through ALA, supporting increased federal monies targeted to youth services. Timing is in our favor here with the attention paid recently to children in poverty and to high schools as armed camps. Why not focus on early literacy as well as on adult literacy? Why not target LSCA monies to useful materials and services for children and young adults rather than (as they have in some states) to esoteric, rarely used microfilm? Why not create federal programs uniting children and young adults with senior citizens, as in a senior advocacy program I recently heard about in Miami high schools? Why not design programs in which YAs serve as mentors to latchkey children and to one another, as in Dr. Gerald Jampolsky's mentoring programs among children with cancer? Why not . . .?

At this point, yet other dragons rear their ugly heads, sounding somewhat like this:

"We're not social workers."

"We don't do it that way."

"We don't have the money, staff, or time."

"We don't get any support."

"It's too risky."

"I tried that ten years ago, and it didn't work."

"I can't do it alone."

Library service to youth started by opening doors and hearts to the offspring of immigrants. We need to do that now. On both coasts, Haitian,

Vietnamese, and Nicaraguan children are storming our shores and our libraries, waiting to be served. Will we learn to speak their languages, and they ours? Will we strive to understand the hidden barriers to service, such as Haitian parents' terror of Big Brother, the computerized circulation system? Can we communicate to them that online registration does not represent death? Can we even explain the notion of the free public library to someone from a Third World country in which books are a rare commodity solely for the rich? Can we reach out and touch the homeless? How?

If ever there was a time to be open to change, it is now. Young adults are in shopping malls, as Audrey Eaglen recently pointed out in a *School Library Journal (SLJ)* article, we need to reach them there. Children are in day care centers. Ditto. Working, single parents have remade the world for children and young adults. We need to build community coalitions to serve them and resolve mounting problems of fractured families. Consider new child and young adult patrons, new technologies, mounting crime, drugs, and teen suicide rates. We need to remember that in offering the gift of literacy we are also offering survival and self-esteem. A recent panel of middle school students in Broward County, including a new immigrant, told a meeting of youth librarians that, above all else, kids need positive reinforcement. "Do you know how often we are put down?" they said. "Do you know how many people tell us we are no good, that we'll never make it? Do you know how hard that is?"

I recall a librarian I knew in the fifth grade who told me that I was a good reader. She said thatI needed something more challenging. That simple act of positive reinforcement took only a minute, but it has lasted me a lifetime.

Which brings me to the way we treat children and young adults in libraries. Over the years, I have heard and seen many things concerning equal treatment of young people. *Scene:* A library guard, frustrated by not making the police force, throws his weight around and verbally abuses a young adult patron. *Scene:* A child, eagerly anticipating getting her first library card, is given the third degree by an unsmiling circulation clerk. *Scene:* A branch librarian glares at a child, addressing only that child's mother. The last scene is from my own childhood. I begged Mother to go to the big downtown library, where there was actually a children's librarian who smiled, was glad to see me, and actually had read some of my very own books.

I am glad that ALA and Econo-clad are in the process of establishing two awards to honor excellence in children's and young adult library service. These twin awards will be given, respectively, to a children's/young adult librarian involved in promoting reading and in using literature with children/young adults. The recognition will go to members of ALSC (children's award) and the Young Adult Services Division (YASD) (YA award) who have developed a unique or outstanding library program for children and young adults. We need to produce more such laurels. The book

In Search of Excellence highlights businesses that succeed through exceptionally high standards. We need to put the spotlight on the many hidden success stories, such as Susan Madden's work with young adults in a Seattle detention center and her mentoring of countless youth librarians. We must focus on unique projects, such as Jane Botham's peace program and display and her annual "Poetry Concert" at the Milwaukee Public Library. We need to examine Carolyn Sue Peterson's mobilization of the entire community in Orlando, Florida (home of Disneyworld, an "excellence" site), to reach children through stories and books.

We need to ask the children and young adults themselves what they want in the way of service. Toy companies use focusing groups of children to discover what they really like. Why can't we do the same? Why can't we go out onto the floor and just listen, or at least ask, basic questions about service? In Louisville, we did this to help design a library facility. With full participation by a young architect, we took a model of the proposed youth areas of a branch library to classes of elementary and middle school students. Young children told us they wanted to be up high (so that they could presumably feel taller) among groups of peers. Middle school students wanted to be alone, against the wall, practically invisible. We designed the spaces accordingly, and it was popular with the client group.

Finally, we need to think big. ALSC, YASD, and Library Administration and Management Association (LAMA) are creating a national impetus for excellence in youth services by offering a series of regional institutes on managing youth services starting in 1990. We hope that teams of youth librarians and administrators will emerge from these meetings with implementation action plans to reenergize youth services on the local level.

We must do more of this combined soul searching and achieve activism, joining hands with our colleagues locally and nationally as well as in the community at large. We need to apply for major grants, as several major metropolitan areas have done recently (Chicago, Philadelphia, New York) and show what money can do. We need to show that we are not powerless but that we are guardians of a trust of children and young adults who are the future of this nation. We need to say that we are proud to serve children and young adults, to have made this our life's work. It's important work. It's about time we realized that we are really dragonslayers.

Note

1. National Center for Education Statistics, *Services and Resources for Young Adults in Public Libraries,* Fast Response Survey System, no. 28 (Washington, D.C.: NCES, July 1988).

Free for All

JUDITH L. WILLIAMS
Director
Jacksonville Public Libraries
Jacksonville, Florida

PATRICIA C. DOYLE
Librarian
Central Library
Jacksonville Public Library
Jacksonville, Florida

Our library is like yours in its commitment to service. The Jacksonville Public Libraries' response to change has been exciting. Our staff is working hard to develop customer-driven services; that is, we define a customer as one who comes to us for a service. However, we need to draw a distinction between excellent service and merely having a product to sell. The concept we want to emphasize is sensitivity to the needs and demands of users. It is important to remember that since we have no real competitors, it is easy for staff to forget that we need to *satisfy* our customers as well as provide a product or service.

Changes in Traditional Services

Traditional services at Jacksonville Public Libraries have been challenged by change:

- The Jacksonville Public Libraries have two literacy programs: parents and tots, and computers and literacy.

- New buildings for main and regional branches have been designed to accommodate new technologies and information services.

- Headquarters (main library) was rearranged to improve access and provide open shelves.

- Fines were eliminated based on value of materials returned and the removal of the psychological barrier of fines.

- The types of media and balance of collection – from informational, to educational, to recreational – vary from unit to unit. Information provision seems to be our unique role. There is a growing sophistication seen in users.

- Technology and automation are making it easier to produce enhanced services.

- In reexamining the mix of professional versus clerical staff, we find that clerical jobs are vastly diminished.

- Competition for funds is constant and productivity-based in a growth economy like Jacksonville's.

At this conference, the "economic value of information" was indicated as a primary consideration for libraries today. Strange words to some, but relevant.

I believe we must be vigilant in guarding against reduction of access to a library's basic services. Florida is fortunate to have a development plan that offers state funds in exchange for *free* provision of all basic library services to its community. However, we must be prepared for the challenges, coming from both inside and outside the library, to recoup the costs of services by passing them on to the customer. This may seem like a tempting solution to the rising price of information services. But we must understand that, although information is valuable, access should be as barrier-free as possible if we are to uphold the long-held, viable tenets of our profession. An informed community, regardless of the status of its citizens, is the best safeguard we have for democracy.

These are critical times. My staff at the Jacksonville Public Libraries has helped me to identify some of the issues that challenge us today:

- Importance of information for survival.

- Competition for funds.

- Economic value of library service.

- Information rich versus information poor; haves versus have-nots.
- Safeguards against information control by any minority interest.
- Librarian/information specialist as the key.

It is strongly felt that the most serious problems are proliferation of fees, contracting of library services, and establishment and assignment of a value to what is done in libraries. American public libraries could be in danger of going the way of British public libraries or federal government libraries.

As Thomas Paine said in 1776, "These are the times that try men's souls." Whether it is nobler to pursue the economic self-interests of this great nation or to strive for the social benefits of each and every individual who constitutes the united strength of this mighty land is the question. The pendulum swings back to those things that were thought to be forever relegated to the nether realm of archaic ideas, eighteenth-century thoughts imposed on twenty-first-century ideology. What can it mean and where are we headed?

The Dangers of Privatization

Thought by many to be the cornerstone of democracy, public libraries must become alert to the substantial threats inherent in any kind of privatization of functions, whether this relates to the charging of fees for specific services or to the wholesale contracting out of entire libraries. Dangerous precedents have already been set as can be seen by many examples in the federal government. One has but to speak with colleagues in federal and military libraries to hear what can only be described as war stories, where the battlefield has little to do with the defense and promotion of honor and integrity but significantly with what is politically the most expedient agenda on paper.

In this age of technocrats and number crunching, most of us are aware and, perhaps, guilty of manipulating statistics to what we perceive to be our best advantage. Governments are no exception to this kind of behavior and, in fact, may be particularly skilled in areas of deception where promoting convoluted ideas frequently warrants reward. As an example, in the state of Florida there have been libraries on military bases that have been contracted out despite the knowledge that the savings in some cases are paper savings only and that actual dollar costs tended to increase. These are libraries as close as Jacksonville and Pensacola.

Libraries in these cases have been trampled on by bureaucracy. Little thought was given to the nature and mission of libraries, but, instead, someone somewhere in the upper echelon of government decided that information was a commodity and service that could be considered as a commercial activity and, as such, should be subject to the vagaries of capitalism. Therefore, federal libraries became targets of contractors' bids.

If we accept the premise that libraries serve the betterment of society, we might make the analogy that libraries are representative of society. If this is so, then let me take the liberty again to quote Thomas Paine: "Society in every state is a blessing, but government, even in its best state, is but a necessary evil; in its worst state, an intolerable one. "At the same time that Thomas Paine was espousing the virtues of freedom, justice, and the equality of man, another voice rang out. That voice belonged to Adam Smith. In "The Wealth of Nations," he said "By pursuing his own interest he frequently promotes that of the society more effectively than when he really intends to promote it." Smith was speaking of economic self-interests, which he felt could advance society more than the promotion of social interests could. Smith's ideology generated considerable controversy that still exists today. For example, there is outrage and alarm being sounded in what was once thought to be a great American mecca, Phoenix, Arizona. Once praised by environmentalists as an ideal city, Phoenix is now plagued by so much pollution and overdevelopment that the media indicate that exodus of a concerned populace is imminent. Yet eminent capitalists scoff at this thought. They say that free enterprise and capitalism will solve the problems of Phoenix; no need for alarm.

So the word *privatization* is increasingly bandied about. *Webster's New World Dictionary of the American Language* defines it as the noun form of *privatize,* which means "to turn over a public property, service, etc., to private interests."[1] It appears as if Adam Smith's concepts have gained renewed energy and acceptance. Those with vested interests obviously condone such action, as do those who are led to believe that privatization is synonymous with cost savings, efficiency, and quality. Those who condemn it know that lower costs and quality may have little or nothing to do with transferring public service over to private enterprise. They do know that what is at issue is a matter of ethics and accountability to an entire nation of people, not something to be swept under the rug or reserved for a select few.

Yes, the word *privatization* may be new–it has been injected with strength and vitality by those who stand to gain the most from its acceptance–but it is not a new concept. Historically, supporters of public library service fought many long and hard battles to provide free access to information for all people, both here and in Great Britain. The eighteenth-century subscription libraries excluded working-class people who could not afford to borrow books. The nineteenth-century saw many controversial issues raised relative to taxing the middle class to support library service to the working class. Not until the twentieth-century did comprehensive and free library service become a reality on a national scale.

It is interesting to note that the Adam Smith Institute is currently using certain historical information about the British Public Library service to promote its case for privatization. The institute claims that growth of libraries relied heavily on private funds.[2] This is true. However, support by philanthropy and turning libraries over to commercial enterprises are not synonomous. Private industry is always interested in the profit motive. It is this interest that is likely to harm those who are least able to pay for information. If the son of a weaver had not had the opportunity to benefit from reading in libraries, he may not have grown up to be one of the most ambitious library benefactors known to us. Who was he? None other than Andrew Carnegie.

The Need for Populism in Libraries

There is no doubt that Andrew Carnegie would be interested in another idea that is currently taking hold across the land in both Democrat and Republican strongholds. Again, like privatization, this idea is not new but has resurfaced from the past. The word for it is *populism*. In its best sense, it means faith in the people. *Merriam-Webster Pocket Dictionary* defines a populist as "a believer in or advocate of the rights, wisdom or virtues of the common people."[3]

Some say that populism offers a progressive alternative to liberalism. It is an inclusive, not a divisive, philosophy. Populists believe that the poor should be given the means to enter the middle class and that people who are most affected should always have the most to say. "Progressive populism starts from the simple premise that too few people in America control too much of the money and power," insists Illinois Congressman Lane Evans, "and they are using it against the vast majority."[4]

This is what some say is happening in Phoenix, and this is what some fear will happen in libraries where fees may become unrestrained, promoting a clear division between the information rich and the information poor. Some public officials and business communities across the country are already recommending that nontax revenue be realized through fees charged for library services. Various departments within the city of Jacksonville are currently being studied in this regard, as is the library.

The Question of Fees

As you may recall from the 1 February 1989 issue of *Library Journal*, a new plan for fees at the Milwaukee Public Library was approved as a result of a recent study by the public policy forum, an organization that analyzes tax trends. It was suggested that fees could be charged for rental of multiple copies of best-sellers and videos, research service for business, and rental of meeting rooms. Other ideas for generating revenue were a restaurant, gift shop, and outreach services such as books by mail. In general, though, it was felt that the study revealed that very few library services can be supported by fees because of legal constraints and economic cost-benefit analysis.[5]

A visceral response to fees is engendered in librarians who take ALA's Library Bill of Rights to heart, for it specifically states that "citizens should have free access to information." If one is to believe in, defend, and promote the standards and ethics of the profession, there seems to be little choice but to oppose fees that deter access to information.

The other side of the coin is that resources are scarce and limited. Information brokers argue that the laws of economics apply to public institutions as well as to private ones. Some say that fees are necessary to provide database services at all. They say that if there are no fees, there can be few technological services.

In the 20 February 1989 issue of *Library Hotline* is an article entitled "Defense of Fee-Based Service in Arizona." Arizona State University has a service called FIRST, which stands for Fee-Based Information and Research Service Team. A private information broker claimed that FIRST represented unfair competition. A panel created by the Arizona legislature to protect small business from unfair competition ruled in favor of Arizona State University.[6] Fee-based services are gaining strength and legitimacy where once they had little.

In this same issue of *Library Hotline* is an article entitled "Tacoma to Provide Federal Contract Assistance to Small Business." The Tacoma Public Library has been awarded an LSCA grant to provide its business community with a collection of materials to assist interested parties in securing government contracts. They also plan to provide workshops in the use of this service and in the bidding process.[7]

It is ironic that government libraries are themselves subject to being contracted out. In Jacksonville a federal library was contracted out to an aircraft refueling company. By their own admission, representatives of this company were looking only for a foot in the door in order to obtain larger, nonlibrary contracts. Obviously, their interests were not library-related. In these days of defense-contracting scrutiny, we as librarians might do well to open our eyes to forces around us that impact our profession–forces that have, until now, remained relatively hidden. This is not a time to cling to the cloistered walls of ivory towers. This is a time to take a stand. Who are we? Why are we here? What must we accomplish? How did things come to be this way?

It is generally thought that, within our generation of librarianship, charges for services began in the 1960s with the advent of photocopiers. Providing free photocopies was not feasible because of excessive popular demand and the resulting cost of operations. Several years later some academic libraries began to charge for interlibrary lending and for the use of their collections by visiting scholars. In the 1970s bibliographic networks appeared, followed by online searching.[8]

Information science branched off from library science, and graduates from these programs became interested in and were encouraged to follow the path of profit, that is, to charge fees for the same services and resources that librarians provided for free.

And so we are in our current state of conflict. Are we a business or a public service? Is it our responsibility to generate income from taxpayers? Or is our responsibility to keep the taxpayer informed of the many constraints within which libraries operate? Perhaps the aid of the taxpayer should be enlisted to monitor databases and services that may overcharge for the sake of profit. Perhaps cooperation should be sought from the private sector relative to communication technologies.

Perhaps governments and libraries should work together more closely in defining what is due to the people. Do taxpayers deserve to be consulted about fees because they believe their tax dollars pay for free service? Why is it that information should cost additional fees, above and beyond tax dollars, and police and fire safety should not? Perhaps those who are in need of police protection or rescue from fire should pay additional fees for this service. What good will it do a community to provide services to protect the physical bodies of individuals without also providing adequate services to promote intellectual, mental, and spiritual growth to these same bodies?

If fees seem to be the appropriate measure to take to provide database services, why not use fees to beef up ailing book budgets? Surely, healthy collections could be built through the imposition of fees on the existing collection. Perhaps small fees should even be charged for entering the library, just as they are charged in parking lots. This would serve a twofold purpose. It would help with operational costs and it would deter undesirables. Perhaps the automated catalog should require a fee. Or perhaps libraries as we know them should be eliminated and replaced with warehouses that rely heavily on robotics and computers for retrieval of materials. Perhaps these should be coin-operated. But then what will happen to the information-poor scholar, the self-taught individual, the future of America?

The February 1989 issue of *American Libraries* ran a photograph of social theorist Amitai Etzioni talking with librarian David Cohen. The caption read, "Etzioni applauded the library profession for placing moral and ethical commitments above economic efficiency."[9] But are we?

Lately in management theory a new buzzword is surfacing. That word is *third-wave management thinking.* In the third wave, chain of command is replaced by networking. Focus on institution is replaced by focus on individual. Flexibility replaces structure. Inspiration is valued more than dogmatic leadership. Affordable quality is replaced by no compromise in quality. Personal growth is valued more than personal security. Making a difference is more important than title/rank/money. The major objective is to build, not to compete.

Theorists claim that adoption of these high-involvement, high-commitment concepts can lead to a 40 to 50 percent boost in production, higher quality control, and better employee morale. Many corporate CEOs, however, are reluctant to pursue any changes that involve power sharing and information sharing.[10]

These third-wave ideas seem to be the very ones that are consistent with the standards and ethics that many of us learned as library science students. Perhaps it is a sign that better days are ahead. Perhaps they are the light at the end of the tunnel.

This is not to say that many struggles do not lie ahead. Many unresolved issues must be addressed, and we are the ones who must address them. To close with a final quote from Thomas Paine: "We have this consolation with us, that the harder the conflict, the more glorious the triumph. What we obtain too cheap, we esteem too lightly; 'tis dearness only that gives everything its value. Heaven knows how to put a proper price upon its goods; and it would be strange, indeed, if so celestial an article as freedom should not be highly rated." As library professionals, we can play a part in sustaining democracy. We can uphold the Library Bill of Rights. We can look for solutions to support the rights of each and every individual who makes up the united strength of this great nation. We can make a sincere effort to provide free access to information, ensuring that the struggles of our predecessors do not end in vain.

Notes

1. *Webster's New World Dictionary of the American Language,* 2d college ed., s.v. "privatize."

2. Macdonald Daly and Gordon Riddel, "Turning Back the Clock," *History Today,* October 1988, 6.

3. *The Merriam-Webster Dictionary*, s.v. "populist."

4. Lewis MacAdams, "Populism Offers a Progressive Alternative to Liberalism," *UTNE Reader*, March/April 1989, 72.

5. Graceanne A. DeCandido, "New Limited Fee Plan for Milwaukee PL," *Library Journal*, 1 February 1989, 18.

6. "Defense of Fee-Based Service in Arizona," *Library Hotline*, 20 February 1989, 2.

7. "Tacoma to Provide Federal Contract Assistance to Small Business," *Library Hotline,* 20 February 1989, 4.

8. James F. Govan, "The Creeping Invisible Hand: Entrepreneurial Librarianship," *Library Journal,* January 1988, 36.

9. "Social Theorist, Amitai Etzioni, chats with David Cohen, Librarian and Longtime Social Activist," *American Libraries*, February 1989, 102.

10. "Third-Wave Management Thinking," *Personal Report for the Executive,* 15 February 1989, 4.

Public Library Service to Special Groups

GERALD JAHODA
Professor
School of Library and Information Studies
Florida State University
Tallahassee, Florida

Special groups will be defined, reasons for offering service to such groups will be discussed, and necessary and sufficient conditions for public library service to these groups will be suggested.

What Are Special Groups?

When I started work on this paper, I compiled a list of special groups. These included, among others, the physically disabled, the elderly, the homeless, the economically deprived, the institutionalized, ethnic minorities, the mentally disabled, and non-English-speaking persons. On reflection, some of these groups are more justifiably called special groups than others, at least in terms of public library service. For the purpose of this paper, special groups will be defined as groups whose members require one or more of the following:

- Material in special format.
- Material in a language other than English.
- Material at a special level.
- A special delivery system for material and services.

The resultant special groups are listed in Table 1. Also on this table are (very rough) estimates of the number of people in these groups. The estimates are faulty for several reasons. For one, they are based on statistics that were compiled at different times. For another, the categories are not mutually exclusive. A person who is functionally illiterate, physically disabled, and born in a non-English-speaking country would be counted as three persons. This factor causes an overestimate, which may be compensated for by underestimates of non-English-speaking immigrants and mentally or physically disabled persons, who may be unable or unwilling to respond to surveys. The homeless, a group that was not included because it did not meet the operational definition of special groups, had two estimates that differed by almost an order of magnitude. The U.S. Department of Housing and Urban Development has estimated between two hundred-fifty thousand and three hundred thousand homeless in this country, while an activist group, the Committee for Creative Nonviolence, estimates that there are about 2.2 million homeless in the United States.[1] It is interesting to note that President Bush used a figure of two million homeless in his 1989 budget message to Congress.

Table 1. Special groups with population estimates

Group	Estimate
Physically disabled (includes hearing, orthopedic, visual, or speech impairments)	44 million[a]
Over age 25 with eight years education or less	19.6 million[b]
Foreign born (not from English-speaking countries)	13.3 million[c]
Institutionalized (includes nursing homes; excludes correctional institutions)	2 million[d]
Developmentally disabled (mentally retarded, severely emotionally disturbed)	6.8 million[e]
Total	85.7 million[f]
Proportion of population	35.5 percent[g]

a. John L. Czajka, *Digest of Data on Persons with Disabilities*, ED 261,519. (Washington, D.C.: U.S. Department of Education, 1984, 2.

b. *Statistical Abstract of the United States, 1988* (Washington, D.C.: Bureau of the Census, 1988), 126.

c. Extrapolated from Ibid., 38.

d. Extrapolated from Ibid., 52.

e. *Interracial Books for Children Bulletin* 8, nos. 6, 7 (N.Y. Council on Interracial Books for Children, 1977): 20.

f. Categories are not mutually exclusive.

g. Based on 1986 estimated population of 241 million, *Statistical Abstract*, 17.

What is Accessiblity?

In a physically barrier free library, a person in a wheelchair would be able to park the car near the library, get to the library via a ramp, and get into the library through a door that is easy to open or, even better, that opens itself. The tables would be the right height, and the aisles would be wide enough to go through with a wheelchair. These and related conditions have been developed for us in the ANSI standards.[2]

But an architecturally barrier free building does not a library make. An intellectually accessible library would obey at least two of Ranganathan's laws of librarianship: Every book its reader, every reader his or her book.[3] The book in this case would be what Louis Shores has called the generic book. [4] It may be a book or a journal article or a videotape or a compact disc or any other format of information. The generic book needs to be in the appropriate format, at the appropriate level, and in the appropriate language.

But material in appropriate format, level, and language does not a library make. It may take considerable effort, both mental and physical, to come to a library that appears strange and intimidating. Thus, cheerful surroundings and a pleasant and friendly staff may make the library more inviting. But, again, a pleasant place to visit does not a library make.

What are Sufficient Conditions?

We have to add one more ingredient to these necessary conditions for library service to special groups: a librarian or librarians with the appropriate qualifications over and above assumed technical competence. Let me suggest three such qualifications:

1. Ability to work with people. This includes all of the people who may come to the library. The librarian should be able to serve the person and not let the person's sight, hearing, speech, or appearance get in the way.

2. Willingness or, even better, eagerness to act as advocate for every individual's right to information, whether it be for coping, for education, for recreation, or for other needs.

3. Willingness or, even better, eagerness to be a change agent and tackle problems that the more cautious would leave alone.

How to Go from Theory to Practice

We have dealt with special groups as abstractions–the foreign born, the functionally illiterate, the physically impaired, the mentally impaired, and the institutionalized, who are entitled to library service. In practice, we deal with individuals and do so typically on a one-to-one basis. Let me get down to hypothetical cases: Mrs. Jones, who is blind, and Mr. Garcia, who knows hardly any English. Mrs. Jones wants to visit her daughter in Omaha, Nebraska, this March, and she wants to know the average temperature of the city during that month. She does not need special service but should be given the average temperature, just like anyone else asking the same query. She certainly should not be referred to the Regional Library for the Blind and Physically Handicapped. Mr. Garcia, who wants to learn English, might be helped with the library's English as a second language tutoring program.

I have two more hypothetical cases: Mrs. Logan, who is once again pregnant, and Mr. Miller, who is the proud possessor of a new microcomputer with a hard disk and utility programs. Mrs. Logan comes to the library with her two toddlers. She needs help opening doors, pulling out catalog card trays, and retrieving material from the stacks. She does not belong to any of the five special groups discussed earlier, but she does need special service. Mr. Miller is struggling with a manual that is not user friendly. It is user hostile, bordering on the fiendish. He is also in need of special service, even though he is not a member of any of the special groups under discussion.

This brings me to my conclusion. Making the library physically, intellectually, and psychologically barrier free and having librarians who know how to work with people, who want to be advocates for an individual's right to information, and who are change agents benefit members of special groups and, as an added bonus, are likely to improve library service for all library users.

Notes

1. Mary Ellen Hombs and Mitch Snyder, *Homelessness in America: A Forced March to Nowhere* (Washington, D.C.: Community for Creative Nonviolence, 1982), and U.S. Department of Housing and Urban Development, *A Report to the Secretary on the Homeless and Emergency*

Shelters (Washington, D.C.: Office of Policy Development and Research, 1984). Both sources cited in Richard B. Freeman and Brian Hall, *Permanent Homelessness in America?* NBER working paper, ns2013 (Cambridge, Mass.: National Bureau of Economic Research, 1986).

2. *Standard Specifications for Making Buildings and Facilities Accessible to, and Usable by, the Physically Handicapped,* ANSI Standard A117.1 (American National Standards Institute, 1980).

3. S. R. Ranganathan, *The Five Laws of Library Science,* 2d ed. (Bombay: Asia Publishing House, 1963).

4. Louis Shores, *The Generic Book: What It Is and How It Works* (Norman, Okla.: Library-College Associates, 1977).

Serving the University Family: Truths among the Myths

PAULA T. KAUFMAN
Dean of Libraries
University of Tennessee
Knoxville, Tennessee

I have been asked to make some remarks today to set the context for our discussion about library service to the university family–students, faculty, and staff. I'm pleased to have this opportunity to talk with you and participate in the discussion, and I hope to live up to the assigned task. This seemingly innocent topic is far from a simple one. I hope to incite your thoughts and our ensuing conversation by making some statements you may not want to hear; you surely will disagree with many of them. My goal is to start us off this morning with a bit of controversy, to play devil's advocate a bit, to get our juices going, and to spark what I know will be lively interchanges.

A Fable

A friend of mine, John Howe, interim university librarian at the University of Minnesota, recently told a story that describes well our current confused understanding of service in the university library, which we can fairly characterize as out of control to some degree. John's story is of a man who finally realized his dream to travel to the Middle East. When there, he decided he wanted to learn how to ride a camel. So he hunted up an old camel driver and asked if he would teach him how to ride. "Of course," said the camel driver. "It's very easy. To make the camel go, say, 'Whew!' To make the camel stop, say, 'Amen.' That's all you need to know."

Well, the traveler thought those commands were odd but easy enough to use. So he climbed up on the back of a great beast, settled down in the saddle, took hold of the reins, and whispered a cautious "Whew!" The camel began to lumber down the dusty road of the small town and set out across the shimmering desert sand.

Things went swimmingly; as the rider gained confidence, he wanted more excitement. So he bent down and shouted a loud "Whew!" into the camel's ear. Instantly, the animal broke into a gallop and off they flew, the desert wind blowing through our rider's hair, visions of Lawrence of Arabia dancing in his head.

The minutes and kilometers raced by, until, looking ahead, the rider saw a sheer cliff with a vast chasm stretching beyond it lying directly in the camel's path. Frantically, the rider racked his brain for the command to stop, but he couldn't remember what it was. Finally, in desperation, he did the only thing he knew to do, which was to close his eyes and pray, ending the prayer with a loud "Amen."

In an instant, the camel skidded to a halt – right at the edge of the precipice. The shaken rider, realizing that he had stopped and was not tumbling headlong into oblivion, slowly opened his eyes, peered over the precipice, and sank back into the saddle with a loud "Whew!"

Well, I don't know if we should measure our ability to deliver services to our university communities – indeed our ability to know what those services should be – with a loud "Whew!" or "Amen." It's my thesis here today that we don't know enough about what we're doing, and to continue on the same dusty road we've been on for the past several years could take us over the edge of the precipice.

Modern-Day Myths

The British author David Lodge has written a number of sharply focused novels about life within the academy. In one of his most deceptively charming books, *The British Museum Is Falling Down*, he uses the following epigraph: "Free or open access can hardly be practised in so large a library as this. As it was once put, the danger would be not merely of losing the books, but also of losing readers."[1]

The British Museum is, indeed, a vast cathedral of learning, and it's easy to see why and how a reader might become easily lost. But, even for those of us who are responsible for operating academic libraries much smaller than the British Museum, today's world of information is so vast and complex that it can lose even the most sophisticated of our users in the intricacies of information identification, access, and management systems. Perhaps in the future, the most successful university libraries will be those that not only have the most access to information but also, like the key to success described by the CEO of a highly profitable information company, get information to users in the most useful form.[2] But that's only a guess. I want to focus this morning on how we know what will be successful.

I think we need to peel back the layers of the protected world in which we've been operating to look at some of the prevailing myths about the services provided by late twentieth-century university libraries. Once we've explored what I see to be the current mythology, we'll look at the role of the university library in the context of some of the changes and challenges facing modern universities, and we'll talk about what will be needed to ensure that the library remains vital to the missions of its parent institution. In doing this, I'll talk briefly about how we might think differently about what university libraries need to do and how they might do it.

The five myths:

1. University libraries provide services to most of the students, faculty, and staff in their institutions.

2. Good service means more, not less; good service is cumulative.

3. University librarians know what their users want.

4. Services are designed for users; OPACs are designed for users.

5. University libraries operate efficiently and effectively for their staffs and their users.

Some of these myths emanate from our professional training, in which our service philosophies are imbued. Others originate from a degree of complacency that we have developed over the past decades when we heard few complaints about our services and when, although we were aware of what the declining relative support levels from university administrations meant, we took little action save to draw attention to the fewer numbers of materials we could acquire, the space required for books, and our need to automate. We fooled ourselves into thinking that we really could continue to provide a full array of high-quality services with relatively decreasing resources. As we saw our abilities to provide materials, and later services, erode, we were slow to draw this to the attention of our university communities, stretching ourselves and our staffs mercilessly in what future historians will surely analyze as an unprecedented era of self-defeating strategies – operating to serve no one very well in the end.

Serving All – The Least Common Denominator Problem

In our attempts to continue to provide high levels of services to all, we have failed to identify those services of greatest importance to our changing university communities, choosing instead, in the most macro of terms, to each deliver basically the same array of services as the other. We've hooked our collective wagons to such trendy developments as bibliographic instruction without assessing their real and relative values to our users. We have built costly undergraduate libraries on the false assumption that undergraduates need different resources than the rest of the university community. And then we have torn down those costly edifices to reunite our collection. We must now come to the table with a different set of assumptions and a different idea of what service to the university community will be in the last decade of this century.

The truth is that we have little idea about what's of most value to our users, both currently and in the future. Lest you think I am painting us all with the brush of stupidity, though, I must tell you that I think we really know what we're doing. We're just trying to do too much without a focused sense of priorities.

It is indeed true that the library is central to the university's activities; some say the library is the heart of the university. My colleague, Carlton Rochell, dean of libraries at NYU, has quipped that the library is the stomach of the university. "Libraries are a university's main means of ingesting the nutrients of scholarship. We take in information. We process it – metabolize it, if you will – so that it can be used by other parts of the academic body."[3] Vartan Gregorian, at a meeting last week, noted that the library has become peripheral in many institutions, and, until it returns to the center, it can't be successful in meeting user needs.

Whether heart or stomach, universities exist to encourage the quest of the human mind for knowledge. Our libraries' major goal, then, is to ensure that the scholarly world maintains control of and access to its knowledge – both old and new.

There will continue to be fundamental changes in the relationships between information providers and users of scholarly information. The course of research and instruction in our institutions has been largely dependent on the availability of information resources and services as determined by the central allocation of institutional funds and decisions regarding the use of those funds by librarians and computer specialists. It is the responsibility of our generation of university librarians not only to determine what the most valuable set of resources and services is to our particular users but also to create imaginative new organizational and delivery structures to ensure that we can continue to provide services of the highest value in the future.

Trends Affecting Service

Two major trends will, I think, be most important for our information users. First, there is the tremendous surge in the communication of the results of scholarly activities. From well-established disciplines to the extension of research efforts to second and third world countries to the emergence of oftentimes fragile new subdisciplinary or interdisciplinary activities is coming a veritable mountain of formal and informal scholarly communications. Most of this output is still in print format; as we reach the twenty-first century, most of the new output will still be in print, although an increasingly large percentage will be disseminated only in digitally encoded formats. Because each one of us is struggling mightily with the problems caused by this situation today, I needn't elaborate further. Suffice it to say that between the increase in the production of the results of scholarship and the rise in the prices of most of that output, the bottom line is that academic institutions will never have enough financial resources to maintain the level of core collections they would like.

The second major trend is the application of technology over a full range of disciplines and more often than not located at our users' workplaces – be they offices, dorm rooms, labs, libraries, or homes. The changes from a strong centralized information support system – the library in the main – to a more decentralized model from the user's point of view, emphasize the increasing importance of connectivity and compatibility. As the network becomes the computer, as the network becomes a major information distribution mode, the administration of information and information technology will also need to be changed. Just as the freedom of information has its limits in privacy, decentralization has its limits in the substitution of confusion or chaos for inflexibility or rigidity. One of our biggest challenges will be to make useful order out of the chaos before the chaos becomes so intense that order will have to rise like the phoenix from the ashes.

As Pat Battin, president of the Commission on Preservation and Access, has reminded us, we must acknowledge that we are faced with applying late twentieth-century technology to what are essentially nineteenth-century institutions – the universities – in creating a twenty-first century educational and research environment.

These changes are indeed profound, not only for the way in which they affect library operations. They have even more significance to the way in which members of the university community do their work and require their information support services. Despite the increasing complexities with which we and our users are faced, when we wade through the rhetoric, we see that we really will continue to perform the same functions that we have done traditionally throughout our history – even though the roles and the ways in which we carry them out will change significantly.

Challenges

The university library's challenges are several.

Anticipating Service Needs

First, we must anticipate and evaluate the changes in our users' use of information and in the changing value they will place on different services. If we don't have the services they want in place when they want them, we become of less importance to them. To put it bluntly, we'll be providing services very few people want the most. To install desired services, we've got to give up doing everything and start doing those things of most importance to those on our campus.

Surviving Stiff Competition

Second, we will be facing increasing competition for funds by other segments of the information infrastructure – computer centers, for one. Three decades ago, universities spent 5-8 percent of their budgets for the library and less than 1 percent on computing. Today, they spend 3-5 percent for the library and 2-5 percent for academic computing. Even though universities are spending equivalent, and often larger, percentages of their total funds for information services, each piece receives less than it requies to do what it defines to be its job, that is, to deliver its services. Each piece must compete unproductively with the other for these very limited funds. Basic restructuring within our institutions is what's needed, but we will not see it come fast. Nor will we see it come unless we're in there pushing and leading the way.

Scholars' Needs: A Gateway to Worldwide Resources

Third, we must be prepared to delivery an ever-changing set of services with extremely limited resources. We must develop our local university library systems to become the scholar's window into the world knowledge management system. And we must be responsible for creating the standards defining the system architecture of that world knowledge management system. And we must maintain browsing access to our print collections.

Training and Motivating Staff to Be Change Agents with Idea Power

The real paradox of technology is that, instead of reducing the human role to one of the cog in the wheel, as myth or fear would have it, the replacement of the simpler and more mundane human activities by machines has created an unprecedented demand for higher levels of information support services and an enormous need for the visionary librarian. This visionary combines flexibility, statesmanship, creativity, an ability to tolerate ambiguity and uncertainty, and human relations skills with the vision to create the future and the guts to take the risks to carry it out. In Rosabeth Moss Kanter's words, ". . . individuals actually need to count for more, because it is people within the organization who come up with new ideas, who develop creative responses, and who push for change before opportunities disappear or minor irritants turn into catastrophes. Innovations, whether in services, market strategies, technological processes or work practices, are discovered not by machines but by people."[4] I'll come back to this point later.

Determining Users' Value

Management in the twenty-first century will be creating, providing, and continuously improving organization systems that, when used by organizational members, ensure the creation of value for the users of the organization's products and services. In other words, to succeed in the future, we must identify what is valued most by our users, discover how the value might be increased, organize in such a way as to ensure success, and, most importantly, build our staffs with people skilled in producing and delivering products and services of value.[5]

If the objective of late twentieth-century organizations is to increase their value to the users of their products and services, then we must understand what value is. By definition, value is what is realized by a user of a product or a service and justifies the sacrifice required. The characteristics we could assign to what might be valued by our users are utility, availability, reliability, ease of use, ease of understanding, affordability, contribution to further outcome, and consistency. Elements that are sacrificed by our users are time, money, energy, space, inconvenience, frustration, ego, effort, and loyalty.

The fundamental responsibilities of managers are (1) continuously knowing what is valued by the user and (2) creating and continuously improving organizational systems to increase user value, reduce user sacrifice, or both. Thus, we must ask the questions we often try to answer – poorly, I might add – through user surveys. Who are our users? What is it they value? Of what value are the services we provide? How is value determined by the user? How can we improve value to the user? What does the user sacrifice? How can we decrease that sacrifice?

Organizational systems are patterns of activities that organizations use to facilitate desired outcomes. They include processes, functions, activities, and tasks and are complex and interdependent. Organizational systems are the means through which value is created and user sacrifice minimized. Systems are generally cross-functional, patterned activities that organizations use to assure desired outcomes. Managers must recognize that they are the ones who determine organizational systems; therefore, they must own and know and improve organizational cross-functional systems. The measure of management's success is the amount of increased value created and user sacrifice minimized by the systems. Organizational goals result when organizational products or services are valued by the user.[6]

Although it is difficult for us to conduct the types of market research undertaken by major corporations or indeed even to measure the value of our services by size of market share, we are fortunate to be operating in communities in which our users are typically not reticent in speaking their minds. In *A Passion for Excellence*, Tom Peters and Nancy Austin estimated that 80 percent of a company's new ideas originate from input generated by its customers. Members of the academy are often quick to tell us what's wrong; this does us no good, however, unless we listen and probe to sort out what they're saying. Timothy C. Weiskel, a practicing scholar and a trained librarian, tells us much, for example, about what's of value to certain scholars in today's environment. In a recent article in *Change*, he warns that librarians may be losing one of their strongest allies–the research scholar. Such scholars are now moving toward creating or expanding their own programs to obtain and manage their scholarly information. This requires, he says, time, money, and, most of all, " . . . commitment that many scholars in the past devoted instead to the major research library itself. As steps toward increased computerization proceed, professional librarians may well want to take the time now to think through and cultivate new forms of alliance with the community . . . to secure their own future success in maintaining their rich collections."[7]

The Future

Once we understand more about what is of greatest value and least sacrifice to our users, our university library staffs will need the ability to conceptualize and develop new systems of access, to understand the research process in a broad range of disciplines, to understand changing instructional techniques and methodologies, and to grasp the need and develop the capabilities for bridging the gap between information in electronic and printed forms. Librarians will also need to continue to assist technologists and computer scientists in applying technologies such as expert systems and artificial intelligence methods.

There are many changes required of our library staffs. First, we need to recognize and accept the fact that changes are occurring, demands are changing, and financial resources will become increasingly more limited. We must understand the need for and be able to carry out creative and nontraditional approaches. One of the major benefits we can provide to our universities is to frame the issues, identify the questions, and suggest strategies for solution. If we don't take the lead in this area, we will be led.

Second, we need to take a closer look at the definition of professional responsibility. We'll need to reorganize, restaff, retrain, and recreate whole segments of our operations. Instead of task-oriented activities, professional librarians will be involved in consulting, teaching, planning, designing, developing, and coordinating activities relating in all ways to the information function; of course, professional librarians must be involved in training those who perform those functions. We will need to combine subject expertise, technical knowledge, management ability, and knowledge of our users with our ability to communicate and forge new partnerships with our academic communities.

How will we be organized to meet the cross-functional challenges I discussed above? There hasn't been a real model of university library organizations for years. Each of us will continue to find different ways to best deliver the services of most value to our individual campuses. Libraries will be different in different institutions. Increasing cooperation through resource sharing and other relationships does not mean we'll look more and more alike. On the contrary, I think different successful university libraries will look and be very different from one another. We will need to be creative and resourceful as we think about information services in the future.

Finally, I'd like to offer a few examples of the skills and talents that I think librarians in universities will be required to have over the coming years:

- *Strong subject backgrounds* to provide substantive assistance in conceptualizing and formulating research strategies and problem definition, database expertise, and thorough and evaluative knowledge of software capacities and availabilities.

- *Strong managerial skills* to conceptualize and manage the changing nature of our organizations, to understand how to translate knowledge of users' needs into services and products, to make hard choices and set tough priorities, and to guide managers toward ownership of cross-functional systems to ensure continuously improving organizations.

- *Political skills* to work effectively within the context of the increasingly complex environment of the university and the even more complex environments of consortia of all types and to be effective lobbyists, both locally and nationally, on behalf of our scholars.

- *Understanding of scholarship and the group we call our users* to be able to understand the nature of the enterprise in which we work and to provide effective stimulation and efficient use of our limited resources.

The ability to deliver comprehensive information services to our academic communities will also require the ability to manage complex technologies within constantly changing environments and with comparatively few financial resources. The unprecedented dependency of faculty and students on technology requires more and more funding and the ability of the institution to respond flexibly to the constantly changing requirements as the human mind interacts with technological tools. Does our past record indicate that our odds of achieving success are great? In many areas, yes. In many others – well, I won't place bets.

Our generation, by sheer accident of history, has both the obligation and the opportunity to reinvent library services in our changing universities. The stewardship of our intellectual heritage is our professional responsibility, and we cannot fail to accept the leadership that is thrust upon us. If we don't, someone else will.

Notes

1. David Lodge, *The British Museum Is Falling Down* (Middlesex, England: Penguin Books, 1981), 87.

2. Andrew Pollack, "Dun & Bradstreet's Bid to Stay Ahead," *New York Times,* 12 February 1989.

3. Carlton C. Rochell, "The Next Decade: Distributed Access to Information," *Library Journal* 112 (1 February 1987): 42-48.

4. Rosabeth Moss Kanter, *The Changes Masters: Innovation for Productivity in the American Corporation* (New York: Simon & Schuster, 1983).

5. G. Harlan Carrothers, Jr., "A Paradigm for Management and Total Quality" (Unpublished manuscript, 1988).

6. Ibid.

7. Timothy C. Weiskel, "The Electronic Library: Changing the Character of Research," *Change*, November/December 1988, 45.

Part 4
Impact of a New Major Facility on Library Services

Samuel Lazerow Memorial Lecture: Breaking Ground in Chicago – Planning the Harold Washington Library Center

JOHN B. DUFF
Commissioner
Chicago Public Library
Chicago, Illinois

In the three years I have served as commissioner of the Chicago Public Library, the one question I am asked most by my former colleagues in the academic world is how does a former historian and university president manage a large public library. I have a stock answer that usually takes this form: There really is not that much difference; the library is, after all, the people's university. One encounters in both arenas dedicated professionals whose lives are devoted to the transmission of knowledge. There are several variations on this theme, depending upon the interrogator, but the response invariably follows the same line.

I have, of late, begun to realize that it would be more accurate if I referred to a letter written over a hundred years ago by Mark Twain. Twain, or Samuel Clemens, as he was then known, had left his hometown of Hannibal, Missouri, for Carson City, Nevada. He found it, to say the least, a stimulating experience. Writing to a friend, he declared, "Carson City is filled with booze, wild women and twenty-four-hour gambling. It is no place for a Presbyterian from Hannibal. So I have ceased to be one."

I too have ceased to be an academic and have become a librarian – perhaps not a very good one but certainly a conscientious one. As the small boy said after being reprimanded, "I may not be totally perfect, but parts of me are OK."

Facts about the Chicago Public Library

It did not take me long to learn some basic facts about the Chicago Public Library. For almost 120 years, the library has made its resources and services accessible to the citizens of the city of Chicago to help meet their educational, informational, cultural, and recreational needs. A major urban public library with over eighty branch and regional libraries, the Chicago library also serves as one of eighteen library systems throughout Illinois facilitating resource sharing among 349 academic, special, and school libraries in Chicago.

Chicagoans have always been keenly interested in their library. Listen to these words from the *Chicago Tribune*: "It is, we are afraid, a radical fault in the average Chicagoan of today that he cares very little for anything but the present moment and what it may bring him . . . that he disdains to be taught, because he does not know how ignorant he is." The *Tribune* urged that this citizen be turned loose "into a good, large, free library, with unlimited freedom to find his way into knowledge after having found the way into his own ignorance."[1]

These comments appeared in 1871, the year the Chicago Public Library opened. In the almost century and a quarter since then, a colorful, exciting, needless to say tumultuous, history has swirled around the library. For the last sixty years, public discussion has revolved around the building of a new central library. As a prominent social historian recently observed, this public discussion has "at times been insightful and useful. Mostly, however, it has been filled with the political melodrama and posturing so characteristic of the great city on the lake."[2]

Fortunately, the issue of the new library has at last been settled. The city council in early 1987 authorized a $175 million bond issue, with the library to be located in the South Loop. An exceptionally successful and well received design/build competition, during which over eight thousand citizens expressed their opinions on the merits of the architectural models presented by five finalists, led to the award of the construction contract to the SEBUS Group and its lead architect, Thomas Beeby. Ground breaking took place in October of 1988; construction is well under way. The structure will rise to its full height – ten floors by the beginning of 1990. The interior (730 thousand square feet) is scheduled for completion in early 1991.

What this magnificent new edifice will encompass and how it will help us to provide a much broader and higher level of library service form a major segment of my remarks. Before turning to the central library, however, I believe it would be instructive to describe how one of our newly constructed branches has increased and improved its service to the people of Chicago.

The Conrad Sulzer Library

In September 1985, the Conrad Sulzer Library, one of the city's two regional libraries, opened on the city's North Side. An enthusiastic group of patrons, politicians, and aficionados of books crowded into the building. Their delight with the new structure caused the editor of *American Libraries* to exult: "It was corny, American, thrilling–the real stuff of libraries . . . my library! Wow–65,000 beautiful square feet of it, plenty to go around for the tens of thousands of folk in this largely blue-collar community at the north end of the city, with its pockets of well-heeled merchants and professionals, struggling slum-dwellers, and down-and-out transients. My cultural center–shared with neighbors of almost every conceivable ethnic background, of all colors and beliefs and ways of life, speaking more than 80 languages."[3] Also designed by Thomas Beeby, the Conrad Sulzer Library has received several architectural awards.

The pertinent question, however, is this: How has it improved library service? First of all, circulation increased dramatically, rising over 60 percent in the first month. The patrons came to enjoy their new amenities and–a most significant point–found more books on the new shelves. They found, in addition, a wider array of periodicals, more and better reference sets, and easier access to materials made possible by a state of the art technology that helped to maintain the early circulation successes. By the end of 1988, Sulzer's circulation of 540 thousand represented almost one-sixth of the branch system total.

The number of patrons has continued to increase. Some days the flow is so intense that there are waiting lines outside of the building. Also, there is greater interest in the general reading, children's, and audiovisual materials. Increasingly higher numbers of secondary and elementary schoolchildren are participating in library programs. The residential community has shown its interest by offering more volunteer hours, supporting programs, and using special collections. The presence of the library has attracted a number of young professionals, and, in the last three years, the property values near the library have increased significantly. As for staff, they are better dressed, their behavior is more professional, they invest more time in helping patrons, and their morale is better than it has ever been.

Truly, the Sulzer library has been a great success; why should it not be? The building is magnificent. It's amply supplied with comfortable and aesthetically pleasing furniture, contains sophisticated audiovisuals and computer equipment, and holds many of the treasures of our culture in paintings, murals, maps, and the like. Yet, Sulzer has something more. An intangible aura permeates the building. This is a place where one can communicate peacefully with books and other artifacts in the joyful pleasures of the mind.

The Harold Washington Library Center

Now, let's turn to the Harold Washington Library Center. Will it duplicate on a larger scale the success of Sulzer? Many architectural *critics* believe it will. Christian K. Laine describes the design as one that "fits so aesthetically, so architecturally comfortably into the city like a warm, familiar glove. Its form, its symbolism, its monumentality and yes its decorative quality–is so profoundly public, so innovative and so urbanistically appropriate . . . the competition . . . together with the selected winner, should be viewed as a positive, and as an all-out urban celebration. Chicago . . . adds another handsome institution to its illustrious list of civic landmarks."[4]

In awarding the architect its 1988 prize for civic design, *Progressive Architecture* commented, "The design expresses the library's public function, and its general aspect, materials, and imagery are intended to evoke other, well-known Chicago buildings."[5] The design of the Harold Washington Library Center sums up a traditional Chicago maxim, which found its most famous and certainly its most pithiest expression in the words of Louis Sullivan: "Form follows function." Sullivan insisted that the use of a building be efficient and uncomplicated, or, to put it in common library parlance, that it be user friendly. The librarians will find no aspect of this building an obstacle to the performance of their ordinary tasks; patrons will enjoy the provision of generous facilities for access to all forms of information. The planners of the library sought "the widest possible accessibility to a growing and changing body of information under the clearest possible physical conditions," as one architect stated. "In a good public building, you should not have to ask your way around."[6] On one hand, this meant recognizing and appreciating the insistence of modern librarians on a high measure of flexibility in their buildings. They ask for a minimum of fixed obstructions and the widest choices in the locations of staff, readers, and books.

We are interested, however, in serving the public as well as in facilitating the tasks of the librarian. Therefore, while the Harold Washington Library will be a flexible building, the designers do not concede that "flexibility itself is the answer to all problems nor that a reading place defined only by a movable grid reference adequately meets the needs of the reader. The program identifies the need for intelligible routing through the building, for a system of organization that reduces the direction giving *load* on the staff, and for a variety of reading environments consistent with the need of supervision."[7]

While I believe that the architects have presented a rational plan to better serve our users without inconveniencing the staff, two features of the new structure, while receiving general public approval, remain controversial. The first is a series of reading alcoves set along the State Street side of the library. The architect contends, "In these formed volumes of space designed to accommodate the individual, the most important traditional activity of the library occurs: reading. Surrounded by surfaces of fine wood and granite, the elegance of the large reading rooms in traditional libraries of the past is recalled in an environment that reflects current library practice."[8] Some librarians, skeptical of the utility of these hard-to-supervise alcoves, predict that another traditional activity, *sleeping*, is more likely to occur in these intimate and introspective areas. Time will tell.

The second controversy centers on the public spaces of the library. The rules of the design/build competition stipulated that each proposal must provide at least thirty thousand square feet of public space. The response to this requirement produced in most cases traditional solutions: a grand entrance hall, spacious reading rooms, or a central courtyard admitting daylight. Architect Beeby proposed a radically different concept for a library. He located the public space at the top of the building. He explains his reasoning this way: "The traditional library courtyard, now agreed to be a constraining interruption in library floor areas, nevertheless was often a much-loved contribution to the public life of the building. Here it is lifted above the body of the library, and is transformed into a winter garden – a unique and exhilarating space of light and trees – a place to read books and eat lunch. A library restaurant opens onto it. Staff spaces surround it on two floors, giving a good working environment with frequent views out, good internal connections and 'front doors' from the winter garden for public access where appropriate."[9]

Critics perceive a certain elitism in locating the public area in what has customarily been known as the executive suite of tall buildings. Is this a deliberate attempt to exclude the street people who have for almost a century used the old library as a warming center from winter winds? At present we are considering ways to ensure that these floors will be truly public spaces.

Let us move beyond design to other interesting features of the library, through which we attempt to improve our service to the citizens of Chicago. An orientation theater close to the library entrance will provide a major element in the development of a user-friendly library. With a constantly running video describing library services and collections, it might be used by even the casual visitor as an introduction and first step to the use of the library. It also will be the first segment of a staff-guided tour for students or other users and will present the broad overview necessary for further in-depth use of library services and collections.

The library's computer connection is designed to allow patron's access to current technology and to support independent learning utilizing a wide variety of contemporary support systems, for example, personal computers, System 80, and Plato Educational/information software packages will also be available, together with a collection of manuals on word processing, spreadsheet programs, and the like. A variety of microcomputers and printers will complete the system. Users will be able to summon staff guidance in the use of equipment, but the emphasis will remain on self-help.

Renderings of the Harold Washington Library Center

A special service within the computer connection will be *Study Unlimited*, a joint project of the library and the Chicago city colleges. It will provide a guided learning program outside the traditional classroom environment. With the aid of videocassettes and other audiovisuals, *Study Unlimited* will offer an independent, self-paced learning alternative to conventional study. Courses may be completed for college credit, for personal enrichment, or for the college credit by examination program.

The learning language laboratory will support the library user endeavoring to learn another language, whether it be English as a second-language or a non-English language. It will also serve patrons who wish to listen to recorded materials from the literature collection–drama, poetry, novels, literary commentary, short stories, and so on. The lab will have twenty-five carrels operated from a single staff-operated console. Learning materials in a variety of recorded formats may be utilized; users will be able to repeat sections of particular interest using controls in each carrel.

A major focus of the central library will be library-related programs and exhibits. Unique and irreplaceable collections of materials such as Civil War books and artifacts will allow the library to present programs and exhibits of special interest to Civil War buffs, even including concerts with instruments used during the Civil War. Original Chicago performing arts material will be the focus of other programs and exhibits, as will other unique Chicagoan collections. Unique and costly book-related exhibits such as an original copy of the Magna Carta will be featured in the new central library because of the advanced security measures that will be available. Programs such as an oral history of Chicago neighborhoods or seminars/workshops for library users and staff will be videotaped in the auditorium with equipment and lighting that permit the highest quality. These videotapes suitable for cable TV will be available throughout the branches.

A satellite dish will allow worldwide TV programs to be received and presented in the auditorium, a unique opportunity for international cooperation in business, government, and the arts.

As soon as the plans were revealed for the Chicago authors' room–a large area dedicated to the city's writers and available for reading, research, workshops, literary events, and meetings of groups like the library club, the Caxton club, and the poetry society–we began to receive requests for reservations. The major collection of Chicago authors' books will be housed in special kiosks outside the room, the more valuable materials in locked cases. Other popular and circulating collections will be placed in easily accessible areas around the escalators and elevators on all division floors. Examples are the social sciences division and the job search/resume collection in the business/science/technology division.

The computer-assisted reference center will represent the latest state of the art for quick and current reference. The use of an online terminal to a computer will be the fastest way to a bibliographic reference or a statistic required by a patron. The product of this service is similar to hard copy indexing or abstracting services. In some cases, it includes statistics or current news information. In addition, research using any other required information methodology will be a part of this service. Librarians will research a project through every possible step: computer-assisted reference, other bibliographic access, books and other materials, and information or materials from other sources. This will include the acquisition of copies of books and periodical articles and professional packaging of the information and materials.

One of the most talked about areas in the new library is the Children's Learning Center, featuring a toddler/preschool area designed for parents and children, an electronic learning center, a small orientation area for class visits, and a large, separate program room. The center will be nineteen thousand square feet. The focal point of the entire service area will be an exciting new service, Nature-Connections, a collection of resources on natural history subjects. Supported by a $700 thousand gift from the Chicago Community Trust to honor two dedicated Chicagoans, the late Herman Dunlop Smith and Ellen Thorne Smith, Nature-Connections will feature not only traditional library resources but also a highly selected collection of "touchables" such as rock samples, shells, pelts, and skeletons. Preeminent institutions such as the Field Museum of Natural History, the Lincoln Park Zoological Society, and the Chicago Academy of Sciences have joined with us in planning this service and are already supporting the effort with programs and exhibits. Nature-Connections in the new library will not only connect children and families with local resources but also establish working partnerships among the city's educational institutions.

A major cultural component of the new library will be a four hundred seat theater consisting of four primary areas: a proscenium stage equipped with full sound and lighting flexibility, film projection, and adequate space; a backstage complex consisting of dressing rooms and storage areas; an audience area with slightly sloped seating for four hundred persons; and a control/projection booth.

We propose two franchise operations in the library. The first is a public restaurant in an area similar in concept to the concourse of the state of Illinois building. It should resemble a restaurant in a museum or perhaps the Broward County Public Library restaurant in Fort Lauderdale, with one or more vendors serving medium-priced upscale food and drinks. The second franchise, the museum store/gift shop, would offer items related to the library, to books, to the literary arts. Those of you who are familiar with the store of the Art Institute in Chicago or that of the Metropolitan Museum of Art in New York should be able to envision the style of operation we are proposing.

Needless to say, collection development in the new Harold Washington library center must take a prominent place, as we plan to improve our service. The success of the Sulzer library derives in large part from efforts in that direction. In a recent article, a somewhat surprised writer described it as perhaps "the finest library of its size in the metropolitan area, because he was able to find such works as Sterling Stuckey's *Slave Culture* and Marina Warner's *Joan of Arc: The Change of Female Heroism*, titles that had evaded him in some outstanding North Shore suburban libraries."[10]

To strengthen the central library collection, we shall concentrate on a last-copy fiction center, a ready-to-read project, genealogy and local history, the home work center, and nonprint materials. Increased attention to the performing arts archive collection will bring together materials from the Balaban & Katz Theater orchestral collection (scores, memorabilia, and programs), video dance and music archives, the Eliza Stigler collection (books about dance), Ruth Page dance memorabilia, come-for-to-sing archives, and the Chicago Musicale Archives.

Chicago has always been one of America's great ethnic cities. The Harold Washington library center will contain more than eighty foreign language collections, with thousands of major works of literature in the original language. In addition, there will be popular *Browsing Collections* in languages other than English, collections that may, in fact, include titles outside of "literature" classifications and that are aimed primarily at the native speaker. These collections include both current and significant retrospective works – collections in Spanish, Russian, and French, for example – and essential current turnover collections – Balkan languages, Vietnamese, and the like. Emphasis will be in purchasing shifts from year to year depending on shifts in immigration patterns and use.

Examples of other subject areas that will be improved substantially are black and Hispanic history and literature, foreign language materials, career and job search information, personal finance, and home improvement information. To comply with the library's designation as "a last-copy fiction center," $600 thousand will be provided over five years by the Illinois State Library. The central library will receive from other libraries in the state of Illinois thousands of fiction titles that would otherwise be lost to posterity.

To improve our made-in-Chicago collection, the Chicago Blues Archives, and other special materials relating to the performing arts and to satisfy public demand and stimulate use of the library, an annual budget increase of $100 thousand will purchase compact discs, video records, audiocassettes and other nonprint materials.

Much thought has been given to improving safeguards against theft of materials. I am not sanguine about the prospective success of these plans. People who are determined to steal usually find a way. It is only small comfort to remember that this problem has long been with us. Daniel Boorstein notes that even monks in medieval monasteries borrowed books and did not return them. We find some interesting warnings in these ancient manuscripts. A special curse was entered against people who mutilated or absconded with them. "This book belongs to the Monastery of St. Mary of

Roberts Bridge," warns a twelth-century scribe. "Whoever shall steal it or sell it or in any way alienate it from this house, let him be forever acursed. Amen." In that same manuscript two centuries later appears a disclaimer: "I, John Bishop of Exeter, know not where the aforesaid house is, nor did I steal this book but acquired it in a lawful way."[11]

Conclusion

Allow me to conclude with a statement of library philosophy first enunciated by the Italian immigrant, Anthony Panizzi, who served as head of the British Museum for thirty-five years in the midnineteenth century. "I want a poor student to have the same means of indulging his learning curiosity, of following his rational pursuits, of consulting the same authorities, of fathoming the most intricate quality inquiry as the richest man in the kingdom, as far as books go, and government is bound to give him the most liberal and unlimited assistance."[12]

We are building the new library in Chicago to give every citizen that "most liberal and unlimited assistance."

Notes

1. Quoted in Neil Harris, "By the Book," *Chicago Times,* November/December 1987.

2. Ibid.

3. Art Plotnick, "Wish You Were There," *American Libraries* (October 1985): 604.

4. Christian K. Laine, "The Harold Washington Library Center," *Metropolitan Review,* September/October 1988, 19.

5. *Progressive Architecture,* The 36th Annual Progressive Architecture Awards, January 1989, 103.

6. The SEBUS Group, *The Harold Washington Library Center: Creating a New Landmark Library,* vol. 1, 1989, D-2.

7. Ibid.

8. Ibid., D-6.

9. Ibid., D-4.

10. Ben Joravsky, "The Local Library: A Branch Grows in Lake View," *Reader* 27 (January 1989): 3.

11. As quoted in Daniel J. Boorstin, *The Discovers: A History of Man's Search to Know His World and Himself* (New York: Random House, 1985), 492.

12. Ibid., 536.

Part 5
Impact of Technology on Staffing

Implications of Technology on Staffing

ANN E. PRENTICE
Associate Vice-President
Library and Information Resources
University of South Florida
Tampa, Florida

Libraries are many things, depending upon your particular expectation, interest, and responsibility. For the person who comes in the front door, they are information places that meet a wide range of needs. That person has little or no interest in how the needed services are provided as long as they are available. For those who unlock the front door, the ways in which information is provided are their bread and butter. They/We are responsible for the multitude of tasks that result in the book on the shelf ready to tempt a reader or the completed online search guaranteed to further a quest for information. For those who pay for the front door and the person who unlocks it and the books and everything else that constitutes a library, there is considerable interest in the satisfaction of the information consumer, the smoothness of the operation, as well as the cost. Local government, the college and university, the business, and the government agency operate under severe financial constraints. Their libraries must function in the most efficient manner possible. As David Penniman said in his keynote address, "Our libraries must demonstrate that they are basic to their enterprise and that they are worth what it costs to maintain them."

Libraries and Technology

Upon review of the literature of librarianship and related areas for this paper, it became apparent rather quickly that when one paired the terms *technology* and *libraries* and/or *librarians*, what resulted was a great deal of information about new technology, from online catalogs and CD ROM to articles discussing how to catalog mixed formats. There were general articles about how technology will change what we do and much discussion about the impact of automation. There was no discussion of how technology, computing technology specifically, actually changes the work place and the work force. Sweeping statements about change were made, but, by and large, librarians expressed their concerns about the changing formats of information and not the changing nature of jobs. Perhaps librarians are more interested in formats. Most librarians did not enter the information professions to be managers, and many library managers are professional librarians but amateur managers who learned their managing skills on the job. This is true of most not-for-profit organizations.

Libraries tend to be organizations that adopt and adapt. Several of our online catalog systems started out as business systems adapted to the library market. Our planning process and budgeting techniques came from the for-profit sector. Our understanding of how technology affects the individual in the workplace, how information changes the nature of jobs, and what we can do to build an information age work place in the library is also coming from outside the library.

The library has regularly adopted technology with varying levels of enthusiasm. Melvil Dewey was a library technology pioneer. He amassed a collection of examples of new technology that ranged from innovative variations on the date due stamp to descriptions of the application of scientific management to library activities. He tried out and tried to incorporate into library operations any number of machines to help out here and there.

Libraries in the 1950s were using microfilm, xeroxing, and taking advantage of the growing reprint business. We became addicted to the Xerox machine, as did our clientele, and xeroxing changed the way libraries were used. We copied a document and took it with us. Internally, carbon paper began to disappear. That is one old technology no one mourns. In the 1960s, computing began to come to libraries. By the early 1970s we were using terms such as *on-line search*, *NLM*, *SDC*, and *Lockheed*. We also learned to say OCLC and began to say RLG and WLN. Our access to collections exploded. We moved into the resource-sharing world. We knew where things were and could locate a book anywhere in minutes. It took and still takes the usual one to three weeks to have the book delivered to the requesting library.

We are now conversant with a wide range of technology that assists in locating information and that provides enormous data banks at our fingertips. Our costs are going up. Feeding and maintaining our online catalogs and our online reference services are expensive. We need more and more staff to do more and more tasks, but do we need all that staff to do all those things? If we look at the way our library is organized, the way work flows in the library, and the tasks that are to be done, very little has changed in the past several decades. Melvil Dewey, if he appeared at your doorstep tomorrow, could walk into the library and in a relatively short time feel right at home. He would be able to take over the operation by the end of the first day, and, from what we know of Dewey, he would indeed take over.

Technology and Staff

There has been some progress toward accommodating to the age of technology. The work has changed and worker attitudes have changed. We are no longer as in awe of technology as we once were. Although computer technology is not quite yet seen as the servant of the library, it has been rejected as its master. Vince Guiliano, a decade or so ago, spoke of the evolution of the work place from the preindustrial model, in which tasks are done manually, to the industrial model with its use of machines (typewriters, xerox, telephone), to the information model, in which information is available electronically and the worker manipulates it electronically. The average library is part of all three ages. Some of what we do is preindustrial, and a number of the tasks that are done manually are done so by choice. We still like to get our hands on reference tools and turn the pages or use selection aids in hard copy. The occasional professor is not the only one who likes to caress leather bindings. I don't know of anyone who still uses "library hand," but there may still be some who would not resist practicing this now archaic art. Much of what we do is industrial. We talk on the phone, use the typewriter, and xerox articles. We are beginning to move to the third phase, the information work place. The online search, fax, and E-mail are all means of moving information electronically.

Because we have been involved to some degree in the development of large systems for storing and accessing data (OCLC is an excellent example), we know what such systems can do. The advent of the online catalog is a good example of how large systems change the work place. Tasks have changed. There is no more ordering of cards. There is much less individual cataloging. Interlibrary loan begins with calling up a screen. Collection development can be done more easily in the context of one's academic neighbors and their holdings. Jobs have changed. Cataloging departments no longer need as many professional personnel to do much of the work. Clerical tasks such as feeding data into OCLC or pulling it off have increased. How is that freed resource, professional time, used? It is spent doing original cataloging of items requiring special attention, getting the archives in shape, attacking the backlog, and cataloging new formats.

Things aren't necessarily done differently. Tasks such as feeding the database are new tasks managed in old ways; in other cases the catalogers are doing their traditional tasks on the materials they had previously lacked the time to catalog. In reference, acquisitions, and elsewhere in the library is an increasing reliance on access to information through large databases for decision making, but the reference department, acquisitions, and circulation are essentially the same departments, structured the same way they were twenty or forty or fifty years ago.

The existing structure has adapted, often quite well, but library organizations are, like most organizations, resistant to real, basic changes. Who is responsible? Most of the studies of organizational change to a technological environment point not to those doing the work but to management. Are those in charge of our libraries representative of MLS graduates of the pre-1970 world when OCLC and DIALOG and other acronyms could be avoided? Are library directors and department heads too busy to look at the changing nature of the structures and tools that they use? No doubt they are because new tools added to old ways of doing things double the job.

How do we get out of this box of trying to manage a work place that is presently on two tracks: the information smart environment where one is comfortable working with the latest technology to retrieve information and the preindustrial environment where staff is still feeding cards manually, shuffling paper, and performing in-house tasks in the same old way that Melvil Dewey would have found comfortable. Dewey, I think, would have a wonderful time in our computer age. He liked to try new ideas and think up new combinations.

The Environment for Change

How can we change the environment, retrain present staff, and anticipate the expectations of future staff? You can't change just one thing at a time; you can't change the original structure only, staffing, or training. The library or the department you wish to change will absorb one aspect of change, surround it, and simply go on as usual. The library administration must create an environment of change. Creating that environment for change must start at the top with the library director. In some instances, the university administration, the board of trustees, or any other responsible agent will hire a librarian to be the agent of change. In other cases the administration will direct the librarian to change the library's environment; in others, the library director will initiate change.

An environment for change is one in which there is the freedom to try new things and discard old ones and in which you are not held back from action because of a fear of failure. When dealing with working environments, we are dealing with people. Not every management technique or change mechanism will work. So what? An environment for change is one in which you know change is work and that it takes effort. An environment for change is one in which you are aware that people resist change because they are unsure of their ability to learn new skills and to adapt to new environments.

No one wants to feel inadequate. The change environment is one in which you know that reconfiguration of the organization, restructuring of jobs, and training will take place.

Often the major difficulty in moving into a work environment that reflects a technologically sophisticated work place is the unwillingness of the manager to change. The individual who has built a power base in the library or department will no longer have that same empire when the organization changes and jobs change. Information will flow differently. The librarian will have to learn new information skills and new management skills. Anxiety levels will rise.

Considerable discussion and research have been carried out in the ways in which technology changes the work place. In the 1950s Leavitt and Whistler predicted that the combination of management, science, and information technology would cause middle management ranks to shrink, top management to take on more creative functions, and large organizations to recentralize.[1] That prediction was generally correct. "Companies indeed reduced the number of middle managers, and computer systems assumed many of the communication, co-ordination and control functions that middle managers previously performed."[2]

Shoshana Zubhoff in her book *In the Age of the Smart Machine*[3] found that what workers do and how they perform tasks have changed radically in recent decades. Clerical work has been restructured dramatically with the application of advanced information technology. Much of the nonprofessional staff in libraries is responsible for clerical tasks, and the majority of library employees are nonprofessionals. How have we restructured their tasks? Have we restructured them? Do we know how to restructure them? Do we know what we are getting into when we restructure? Do we have a choice? Zubhoff says, "Choices that appear to be merely technical will redefine our lives together at work . . . a powerful new technology, such as that represented by the computer, fundamentally reorganize the infrastructure of our material world."[4] It eliminates old alternatives and creates new ones.

We have moved past our fears that the machine would dominate the work environment, although in many areas it often does. We are moving from the machine-centered work place where keeping the machine running was the first duty of the worker, to an uneasy relationship in which the needs of machine and worker were of equal importance, to an environment in which the machine is a tool to be used to accomplish the task. In our stages of absorbing computing technology, are we going through stages of technological acceptance similar to those experienced when the printing press was invented and turned the information world as it was in 1453 upside down? The printing press freed the scribe and made the scriptorium obsolete. The computer freed the catalog clerk, the acquisitions clerk, and numerous other individuals in the library. Or are they free yet? Are they doing both old and new tasks? Are their online record-keeping activities an add-on? Have we really looked at those jobs and those departments with a view to simplifying the work flow? Do these individuals have the skills to succeed in the more technical environment? Does the librarian have the skills to reconfigure the work place? Does the librarian need a little help?

The Technological Environment

Let me suggest a number of steps toward achieving the technological environment that we have no choice but to achieve:

1. Library managers need to understand what the technologically smart work place is and how it can be developed. I doubt that we have the expertise necessary to provide that understanding in our ranks. There are a number of individuals, particularly in business schools such as Harvard and the University of Virginia and in industry at IBM and AT&T, who are defining the technologically smart work place. We need to be involved with them and learn from them how to configure our libraries.

2. Within our libraries, we should review the work flow, the tasks of each individual, and the ways these tasks contribute to the work flow.

3. We must involve all workers in the tasks of reviewing and redefining their jobs. I can hear some folks muttering, "She wants even more meetings."

4. We must learn what barriers may exist. Are they organizational, personal, or educational? How can these barriers be removed?

5. The planning and evaluation process most librarians have in place is a means of reviewing what is done. A parallel process needs to be put in place to review how and why things are done. The two are interdependent.

People work hard and they work harder but not necessarily smart and smarter. As business becomes more successful in applying technology to the work place, workers and managers will become increasingly critical of individuals and organizations who are not working smarter, particularly if it costs money that comes from their tax or tuition dollars.

The key to change is retraining. Our work place is a renewable asset, renewable through retraining. Learning new skills benefits the individual through personal satisfaction, performance improvement, or dollars. Some would be apprehensive because you "can't teach an old dog new tricks," but we are all learning in this new environment and have no choice but to learn if we wish to stay employed. Retraining is cheaper than hiring new people, and the library has an obligation to keep good people.

Computer-based technology mandates training and retraining. Every upgrade requires training. Employees in a technical world are learning every day. They master one word-processing package or one database manager only to receive a new version they must learn.

Who will do the training and the retraining of clerical workers, technical personnel, and professional staff? For support personnel, much of it will be in house with some assistance from vendors. Most library staff development groups function in a preindustrial to industrial mode, not an information mode. Old teaching methods are used to teach new technologies. We can improve and extend training through techniques such as computer assisted instruction. For professionals – and we will have fewer professionals – we will rely on existing supports such as conferences focused on take-home techniques for planning, restructuring, and managing and on formal programs sponsored by professional schools and vendors.

Conclusion

Libraries are now in a dual mode, doing work that can be done in more efficient ways using technology and learning and applying techniques that will allow them to work more efficiently. We need to sort out tasks, set directions, and move ahead before we exhaust ourselves and our staffs. Libraries are information places that provide services basic to our educational world, our economic base, and the enhancement our daily lives. They are also organizations that need to run smoothly and economically.

The research for my dissertation was on the subject of money and funding for libraries. Several people said, "Who cares about that?" Now everyone cares. For some time, we have heard dollars, dollars, dollars in nearly every presentation. In the past three or four years, I've been looking at the work force in the library, at how workers do their jobs, and at how those jobs and the organization itself can be reconfigured. No one has said, "Who cares?" But neither do I see many information professionals exploring this area. Many people during this conference have asked "Why shouldn't the library be an innovator in technological development?" We should. We should also be leaders in organizing our work force and managing technology in an efficient and cost-effective manner.

Notes

1. Harold J. Leavitt and Thomas L. Whistler, "Conversations with Leavitt and Whistler" *Harvard Business Review* 66, no. 6 (November-December 1988): 33.

2. Lina Applegate, James I. Cash, Jr., and D. Quinn Mills, "Information Technology and Tomorrow's Manager" *Harvard Business Review* 66, no. 6 (November-December 1988): 128.

3. Shoshana Zubhoff, *In the Age of the Smart Machine: The Future of Work and Power* (New York: Basic Books, 1988).

4. Ibid., 5.

Information Specialist: Modern Day Librarian or New Professional?

ELIZABETH SMITH AVERSA
Assistant Professor
College of Library and Information Services
University of Maryland
College Park, Maryland

The purpose of this paper is to discuss whether or not an information specialist is a modern day librarian or a new professional, and, if they are different, to identify the functions of their work, the attributes of their viewpoints, and any other relevant aspects that might set workers in the two groups apart.

What Is an Information Specialist?

Before exploring whether or not an information specialist is an updated version of a librarian or a member of an emerging profession, one must answer the question, "What is an information specialist?" A search of the literature of library and information science reveals several important points. Consideration is needed of both what is present and what is not included in the literature.

First, it appears that there is no generic definition of an information specialist. This state of affairs makes the task at hand all the more difficult, but the problem is not insurmountable. Consider what is available from the literature.

In a study that was mounted a decade ago, Don King and others from King Research and the University of Pittsburgh identified six categories of what they termed information professionals. These were information theorists or information scientists, information systems specialists, information intermediaries, information technologists, managers of information services, and educators and trainers of information workers. The same researchers also named nine different functions performed by information professionals and listed an array of occupational titles that has been applied to individuals who perform the functions named. Two features of the lists of occupational titles are important to note.

First, the occupational titles include many that we find on organization charts of libraries as well as on the organization charts of nonlibrary institutions and enterprises. For every function of information work listed, at least one of the occupational titles is typically library-oriented.[2]

Second, and even more interesting, is the fact that there is no category, either functional or titular, called information specialist in this scheme. The simple fact that this category or title is absent from such a thorough listing boosted curiosity and provided energy for a continuation of the literature search for at least a working definition of information specialist.

Jane Spivack, in *Careers in Information,* does provide some definitions and an attempt to differentiate between information professionals, information scientists, librarians, and information specialists.[3] Spivack's categories form a hierarchy, with the category information professional encompassing the other three titles. She goes on to define the others as follows:

> *Information Specialist.* This broad category of information professionals includes people who are not generally working in traditional library settings, although they may very well be using library skills in their work. As already noted, they are primarily processing information using new technologies, and they are more concerned with the transfer, analysis and use of information than with the storage and protection of collections. Information analysts, information researchers, information managers would all come under this heading.

> *Information Scientist.* As used in this book, information scientist has a narrower meaning than one sometimes encounters elsewhere. Here it is confined to someone concerned with the nature of information itself, studying how information is generated and transferred from one source or format to another, how people perceive of and use information. Information scientists are interested in research and sometimes teaching. They work in colleges and universities or for companies such as IBM, Wang, or the Institute for Scientific Information, which maintain research programs to develop new systems. . . .

Librarian. For the purposes of this book the term "librarian" refers to a specific sub-type of information professional who works in a library and performs primarily library-related tasks."4

It is easy to take issue with Spivack's definitions unless one is willing to use them only as working definitions, not as absolutes. Clearly, today's librarians use new technologies to process information. Online retrieval services with downloaded files reformatted via word-processing software, online ordering of documents, and the use of fax to gain instant access to paper copies of materials held around the block or across the globe are just three of many new technologies being used in public libraries throughout Maryland. The individuals who perform these tasks work in libraries, call themselves librarians, but are more "concerned with the transfer, analysis, and use of information than with the storage and protection of collections."[5] Does this mean they are information specialists instead?

Similarly, one could argue that the very tasks Spivack says are performed by information specialists are library-related tasks frequently performed in libraries but sometimes performed elsewhere. Does my answering what is clearly a reference question from my home make me an information specialist just because the task is not done in a library? Taken to its logical conclusion, the place-of-work argument leads me to ask if I am no longer a librarian because I am no longer employed by a library.

Leaving Spivack's definitions and moving to more recent works, one finds two British publications that focus on the problem from different perspectives. The first of these is Nick Moore's *The Emerging Markets for Librarians and Information Workers.* Moore investigated for the British Library Research and Development Department the market for librarians and other information workers in the United Kingdom as part of a major study of the library and information work force.[6] While Moore's methodology involved using newspaper and journal want ads and analyzing the jobs listed for their appropriateness for library and information workers, the contribution of his work to the present attempt to define the information specialist is the categories he identifies for library and information work. Moore identified ten types of work:

1. Library work.

2. Information work.

3. Research and information.

4. Information technology.

5. Indexing and abstracting.

6. Servicing of the information industry.

7. Advice work.

8. Public relations.

9. Management information.

10. Records management.

While some of Moore's categories are distinct one from another, some demand attention. Library and information work are defined as follows: "Library work–Jobs involving library, as opposed to information, skills or firmly based within a unit described as a library. Information work–Jobs requiring the fairly traditional skills of an information worker and usually based within an information unit or service." Finally, the category "servicing the information industry" includes "posts in the firms and organisations which service and support the overall information industry, for example bookselling and publishing when they were aimed specifically at the library and information market, bibliographic data-base suppliers and library automation service."[7]

Moore's categories illustrate the slippery problem of defining terms such as information specialist or even information work. As with the King study, Moore does not use information specialist as an exemplary job or occupational title. Moore's findings regarding the role for library and information science workers in the ten types of positions identified are discussed below.

A second British study reveals several points that are helpful in defining titles and roles within the information professions. Margaret Slater's work, like Moore's, was carried out for the British Library Board. Entitled *Careers Guidance and Library/Information Work*, the work attempted to find out how career advisors at high school and college levels handle library/information work.[8] This study is important to the present task in that it is one of the few studies that show how nonlibrarians and noninformation workers perceive the field.

Slater's respondents in the study were able to distinguish three different "strands" within information work: traditional librarianship, "non-technical but specialist information work," and information science. These occupy different positions on a continuum, with librarianship seen as service-oriented and people-slanted and information science as less people-oriented and more concerned with profits, cost-effectiveness, and the provision of support services. Between the two, Slater's data suggest, is that gray area of nontechnical information work: advice workers, special interest information providers, and the like. Importantly, the career advisors felt that in this middle area of information work would be the greatest growth and opportunity.[9]

Slater's respondents, none of whom were librarians or information professionals, called for a unifying occupational title to describe all of the strands identified. Information specialist was the preferred term. But as Slater observes, ". . . the label for a professional does not translate so easily into a label for a profession. . . . Any discrete discipline . . . could legitimately claim to be an information specialisation, particularly now in this information sensitive era. . . . So a geologist, lawyer, or social anthropologist could claim, among other things, to be an information specialist."[10]

Two additional resources were brought to bear on the problem of defining the information specialist. Lois Lunin once defined an information specialist as one who "studies, executes or controls the gathering, evaluation, organization or transfer of information, usually in a specific discipline or field such as chemistry, psychology, education or marketing."[11] She goes on to distinguish the activities and types of employing organizations where information specialists work. The only library type listed in her table entitled "Types of Organizations Employing Information Specialists" is the special library. Again, some public librarians in Maryland would take issue with this. Workers at Enoch Pratt Free Library in the Maryland collection, searchers in the Montgomery County system who deal with health and environmental information, and business librarians in several counties may be specialists in certain types of information, but they are indeed librarians as well.

Finally, a search of the Department of Commerce publication *Dictionary of Occupational Titles (DOT)* confirmed that there is no formal occupational title for information specialist.[12] Even so, it is useful to put the several library and information-related titles into context as *DOT* classifies them. Each occupational title in *DOT* has been assigned a unique nine-digit code that differentiates titles one from another. The first three digits signify occupational group, the second three are "worker function ratings of the tasks performed in the occupation" and relateg to data, people, and things, and the last three digits indicate the alphabetical order of titles within the code groups.

DOT assigns number 10 to "Occupations in Museum, Library and Archival Sciences," number 100 to "Librarians," and 100.117-010 to "Library Director." Class 101 is assigned to "Archivists," and 102 to "Museum Curators and Related Occupations." "Occupations in Museum, Library and Archival Sciences, Not Elsewhere Classified," includes 109.067-019, "Information Scientist." The category also includes "Research Assistant," "Shelving Supervisor," and Armorer." Other occupational groups, including systems analysts, programmers, and others often associated with information science, or the work of the elusive information specialists, are nowhere near either librarian or information scientist classification codes.[13]

Finally, the definition of information scientist in *DOT* encompasses some of the work that Spivack attributed to the information specialist. Lunin's suggestion that the information specialist would know a specific discipline or field is mirrored in the last sentence of the *DOT* definition for the information scientist: "May specialize in specific field of information science, such as scientific or engineering research, or in specific discipline, such as business, medicine, education, aerospace, or library science."[14]

It is clear, then, that information specialist is a job title that is difficult to define. Margaret Slater sums up the search for a definition this way: "As people allegedly in the communications business, library/information workers have not created the necessary clear definitive terminology, nor the mutually exclusive occupational labels to enable themselves or others to discuss this topic properly."[15]

Having put to rest the notion of a clear definition, one is free to consider the relationship of librarianship to the practice of information specialization or to the information profession, broadly defined.

The argument over whether an information specialist is a librarian or not brings to mind the children's saying, "Sticks and Stones can break my bones, but names can never hurt me. . . ." I'm not sure that this is the case if one with a so-called library background presents the traditional image in the job search or interview in a nontraditional setting. On the other hand, I believe that most well-educated and up-to-date (excellent) practitioners of librarianship can market themselves as one brand of information specialist. The brand has to do with academic background and additional training.

What Are the Roles of Information Specialists and Librarians?

If one accepts the assumption that there are differences between librarians and information specialists, however defined, then one must identify the overlaps and gaps in the work, skills, values, and attitudes of workers in the respective occupations. Differences can be classified into two groups: differences in the individuals performing the work and differences in the work itself.

In looking at the individuals performing the work, we have a large literature to support what should be included in the librarian or information specialist bag of professional tricks. Consider background knowledge, technical skills, and the values and attitudes of the practitioners.

Jose-Marie Griffiths has outlined competencies for information professionals. She defines competencies as comprising one or more of the following components:

Knowledge – of librarianship and information science and of specific subject area (e.g. chemistry, law); skills – cognitive, analytical, technical, interpersonal, and basic literacy/numeracy; and attitudes – toward the profession and related to motivation.[16] While these competency areas are broad, they provide a framework for thinking about specifics required. Richard Sweeney proposed six new competency areas for public librarians:

1. Managing information technology, or knowing the technical limits of a new technology, as well as knowing the potentials for its use.

2. Knowledge of the state of the art in technology, both library technology and the technology being used in other settings.

3. Knowledge of emerging technology–what is on the horizon–so that the librarian can plan for the future.

4. Knowledge of users' information-seeking behavior and knowledge of methods for finding out about this.

5. Understanding "societal issues" involved with information technologies: copyright, privacy, intellectual freedom, and the like.

6. Knowledge of ways to build knowledge bases.[17]

The competencies sound very much like those that Lunin discussed, but hers pertained to information specialists, not necessarily to librarians other than those in special library settings. Along with the subject area and technical skills required, Lunin proposed that certain personality traits characterize the information specialist. Characteristics such as intellectual curiosity, an analytical mind, sound judgment, knowledge of users, and, of course, a sense of humor are wanted not only for the information specialist. These characteristics are needed for librarianship and also for every occupation from McDonald's food preparer to physicians, politicians, and even university professors.

Others have proposed skills and attitudes befitting various types of information professionals, specialists, or librarians. Janice Sieburth proposes, in her recent book on online in academic libraries, certain "searcher skills," which include good interpersonal skills, listening skills, creative thinking, persistence and patience, problem-solving ability, flexibility, and interest in professional development and continuing education.[18] Again, what employer would not want employees possessing such "skills"? And further–just to press a point–is an online searcher an information specialist or a librarian?

Janette Caputo's *The Assertive Librarian* addresses the issue of the librarian's image and what assertion, as a learned behavior, can contribute to the librarian's work life.[19] The mere presence of such a title indicates the continuing concern, in this field, for dealing with our own competencies, both behavioral and technical.

As for the technical skills required, we have heard much about the technical, particularly computer-based, skills required of the information specialist. Sweeney tells us that these skills are required of the public librarian now, and, if his advice is not enough, Danuta Nitecki, in a look at public service job ads for libraries in 1983, found there was already a demand for technical knowledge and skill. Out of fifty advertisements, Nitecki found, almost half stated that applicants should possess the ability to perform "computer-assisted services" as a job requirement.[20] That was five years ago, and the demand for such skills has not diminished.

Beyond being able to utilize the new technology in information work, recent attention has focused on needing to manage that technology, just as information specialists and librarians have managed other technologies in the past. The publication of *The Library Microcomputer Environment: Management Issues* and *Management of Online Search Services in Schools*[21] indicates the growing market for materials on how to manage, as opposed to how to do it, in relation to new information technologies.

Finally, something must be said about values and attitudes. It has been suggested that information science and librarianship converge on their shared belief that information is an important and valuable phenomenon, both to individuals and to the whole of society.[22] The study of information and of the people who use it are the basis for the work done by both sets of information professionals. A. J. Meadow, in editing *The Origins of Information Science,* a book of basic papers in the field, included in each of four major sections (Growth of the Literature; Citations and Their Use; Statistical Regularities in Communication; and Publishers, Libraries and Readers) at least one paper that came directly from library practice.[23] Clearly, it is the shared values and attitudes, about information and users that make the line between library work and information work so difficult to draw.

Perhaps it is easier to simply describe what librarians and information workers look like, rather than to consider what they do or what they value. Slater suggests that librarians are more likely to be female, to be younger, to have an MLS or similar degree, to have a humanities or social sciences background, and to see themselves as people-oriented. Slater's information workers were more apt to be male, to be older, to have subject specialties, to come from fields in science and technology, and to perceive themselves as problem solvers.[24]

The second way in which differences can be considered is with regard to the tasks performed and the place in which the work is performed. Those issues were introduced in the first part of this paper, so further attention will not be given to the issue, except to say that the work performed is frequently the same, whether the job holder is a librarian or an information specialist. The place in which the work is performed, the work environment, appears to have a great bearing on the occupational title given to workers. What this suggests is that librarians are still perceived as attached to the institution;

information specialists, performing the same tasks, are not perceived as institution bound.

The distinction of titles by work place, by the way, is not made without hazard. Eli Oboler struggled with the distinctions between libraries and information centers in much the same manner as we have struggled here over occupational titles.[25]

Alternative Careers: Is It an Issue?

For those wishing to make career moves, say from one institution (a library) to another (a corporation or advertising agency) or from one occupation (librarian) to another (information specialist), there are opportunities and some cautions. Several books have been published about what can be done with a library degree, and others have cautioned that certain retraining may be required. Moore suggests, for example, that librarians hoping to get into information technology should expect to compete for jobs with "computing professionals who may well appear to employers to be much better equipped for the job . . ." and that "the way to succeed is first and foremost to obtain a graduate level qualification in computing science."[26] In changing work environments, candidates must know what they know, how they can meet a need of potential employers, and how they should market themselves. If the job requires greater expertise than a candidate can deliver, the alternative career may not become a reality.

Slater suggests that the concern for alternative careers is symptomatic of deeper questions, deeper than can be answered in this paper. What is the aim of library and information science? What is the niche?[27]

Concern for alternative careers may also be based on the fears of librarians that there are more librarians than positions for them to fill. A study of articles and books about alternative careers might reveal more attention to the subject when jobs are scarce. Now we are seeing the opposite in certain areas and types of libraries. Will we see information specialists attempting to enter the ranks of librarians as a result? Redirection within the information professions should be possible with training, retraining, and continuing education. Just as a dentist moves from general practice to orthodontics, so should a librarian be able to move to a more specialized position or another area of information work. The cost of moving within the field will depend upon market demand and the ability of individuals to market their skills.

The Opportunity of Information Work

I promised to reveal the opportunity of an expanded future for the librarian and information specialist. So far, the word has been less than cheerful. We have not been able to define information specialists or their work. The literature reveals that, in many areas, librarians and other information specialists have to compete with other perhaps more narrowly trained workers. We have been inarticulate about the work we do and the workers required to do it. So what opportunity is there?

First, it is clear that it is much more difficult to define the unique aspects of an information specialist's work than those of a librarian's work. While an information specialist *may* be interested in bibliographic information, librarians without fail *are* concerned with bibliographic data. Librarians are always concerned with recorded knowledge, regardless of form or format. The information transfer chain or knowledge production cycle cannot function without a mechanism for dealing with recorded knowledge. Librarians are uniquely qualified to design, evaluate, improve, and operate that mechanism.

Second, the information professions are reportedly multidisciplinary, combining methods and practices from computer science, engineering, psychology, education, and other areas of study and research. It is interesting to note that this is often perceived as some sort of new idea; it is not. Librarianship, when practiced properly, has borrowed methods and approaches from many other fields and, even more importantly, has *contributed* to every field of endeavor. Bibliography and research assistance provided by librarians to scholars in universities and research centers are but two areas where librarians have taken from and have contributed to other disciplines.

Third, both information specialists and librarians are concerned with matching information with users, or those who need information. The need to provide individualized information services and to know the user has been recognized in librarianship for decades, and in information work as long as the specialty has existed. The unique aspect of this for librarians, particularly *public* librarians, is that the user can be known "from cradle to grave." The librarian in the public library is unique in that he or she will serve multiple information needs of the patron over time. Although we are keenly aware of that formal knowledge production cycle, we cannot forget the unique niche we fill in serving patron's recreational, survival, and other needs–needs that probably never result in a publication or any citations at all.

Fourth, the librarian brand of information specialist can be an advocate for free access to information for all our publics. We believe in the value of information and attempt to act on our belief that information can improve lives. While this belief may be shared by journalists, our advocacy methods differ; both are needed.

The final unique aspect of our part of the information professions is institutionally oriented. It is the work place called libraries, archives, and special collections. These institutions have certain features not found in business firms, universities, and other agencies. Librarians, with an understanding of these institutions' missions and goals, their historical place in our culture, and their day-to-day activities, are able to provide leadership for the management and development of the institutions and their services.

Conclusion

What then is the answer? Is an information specialist a modern day librarian or a new professional? I believe that the information specialist (and the related profession, information specialization) has yet to be defined. I am not sure that it will ever be defined. If it is, the modern day librarian will help to write the definition, just as librarians helped to define information science and its precursor, documentation.

This is not to say that specialists in various types of information do not exist. They do. Medical, legal, scientific, and government information specialists do serve specific user groups or deliver specialized information, but these are not general, nonprefixed information specialists. The closest thing we have to a general information specialist is indeed a modern day librarian.

It has been said, "If a practitioner wishes to improve his occupational status, he must adopt one of three strategies: (1) leave his occupation for one of higher status; (2) increase his status within his occupation; or (3) improve the status of his occupation."[28] I believe that the author was correct. I question the appropriateness of a fourth strategy that our concern with occupational titles suggests, that is, change the name of the occupation. Librarians will help to determine if such a strategy is adopted.

Notes

1. Donald W. King et al., "A National Profile of Information Professionals," *Bulletin of the Society for Information Science* 6 (August 1980).

2. Ibid.

3. Jane Spivack, *Careers in Information* (White Plains, N.Y.: Knowledge Industry Publications, 1982), 4-5.

4. Ibid.

5. Ibid.

6. Nick Moore, *The Emerging Markets for Librarians and Information Workers* (London: The British Library Board, 1987), 1-159.

7. Ibid.

8. Margaret Slater, *Career Guidance and Library/Information Work* (London: The British Library Board, 1986), 1-165.

9. Ibid.

10. Ibid.

11. Lois F. Lunin, "The Work of Information Specialists," in *Careers in Information*, ed. Jane F. Spivick (White Plains, N.Y.: Knowledge Industry Publications, 1982), 25-50.

12. U.S. Department of Commerce, *Standard Occupation Classification Manual* and *Dictionary of Occupational Titles (DOT),* 4th ed. (Washington, D.C.: Government Printing Office, 1980).

13. Ibid.

14. Ibid., 72-75

15. Slater, *Career Guidance and Library/Information Work*, 1-165.

16. Jose-Marie Griffiths, "Competency Requirements for Library and Information Science Professionals," in *Professional Competencies – Technology and Librarian*, ed. Linda C. Smith (Urbana-Champaign: University of Illinois Graduate School of Library and Information Science, 1985), 5-12.

17. Ibid.

18. Janice F. Sieburth, *Online Search Services in the Academic Library – Planning, Management, and Operation* (Chicago: American Library Association, 1988), 197-214.

19. Janette S. Caputo, *The Assertive Librarian* (Phoenix: Oryx Press, 1984), 1-33.

20. Danuta A. Nitecki, "Competencies Required of Public Services Librarians to Use New Technologies," in *Professional Competencies – Technology and Librarian*, ed. Smith, 43-57.

21. Sheila S. Intner and Hane Anne Hannigan, *The Library Microcomputer Environment: Management Issues* (Phoenix: Oryx Press, 1988), vi.

22. Thomas J. Galvin, "The Significance of Information Science for the Theory and Practice of Librarianship," *Libri* 34 (1984): 81-87.

23. A. J. Meadow, ed., *The Origins of Information Science* (London: Taylor Graham and Contributors, 1987).

24. Margaret Slater, "Alternative Careers for Library-Information Workers," *ASLIB Proceedings* 36 (June 1984): 227-86.

25. Eli M. Oboler, *To Free the Mind: Libraries, Technology, and Intellectual Freedom* (Littleton, Colo.: Libraries Unlimited, 1983), 45-60.

26. Moore, *The Emerging Market for Librarians and Information Workers*, 1-159.

27. Slater, "Alternative Careers for Library-Information Workers, 277-86.

28. L. Carrol DeWeese, "Status Concerns and Library Professionalism," *College and Research Libraries* 33 (January 1982): 31. Quoted in Lester Asheim's "Librarians and Professionals," *Library Trends* 27 (Winter 1979): 225-58.

Bibliography

Introduction

"Serving the Public – Philosophy, Attitude, and Commitment"

Penniman, W. David. "Database Users: The Industrial View." *The Canadian Journal of Information Science* 12 (1987): 5-14.

_____. "Information Professionals in the 1990's." *Bulletin of the American Society for Information Science* 15 (February/March 1989): 25-26.

_____. "On Their Terms – Preparing Libraries for a Competitive Environment." *The Bottom Line* 1 (1987): 11-15.

_____. "Tomorrow's Library Today." *Special Libraries* 78 (Summer 1987): 195-205.

Penniman, W. David, and Donald T. Hawkins. "The Library Network at AT&T." *Science and Technology Libraries* 8 (Winter 1987/88): 3-24.

Reference Services for Today and Tomorrow

"Traditional Reference Services in Today's Library"

American Library Association. Reference and Adult Services Division. Standards Committee. "A Commitment to Information Services: Developmental Guidelines." *RQ* 18 (Spring 1979): 275-78.

Katz, William A. *Introduction to Reference Work.* Vol. 2, *Reference Services and Reference Processes*. 4th ed. New York: McGraw-Hill, 1982.

Monroe, Margaret E. *Library Adult Education: The Biography of an Idea*. New York: Scarecrow Press, 1963.

Murfin, Marjorie E., and Lubomyr Wynar. *Reference Service: An Annotated Bibliographic Guide*. Littleton, Colo.: Libraries Unlimited, 1977. *Supplement 1976-1982*, 1984.

Rettig, James R. "Reference and Information Services." *ALA World Encyclopedia of Library and Information Services*. 2d ed. Chicago: American Library Association, 1986.

Rothstein, Samuel. *The Development of Reference Services through Academic Traditions, Public Library Practice and Special Librarianship*. ACRL Monographs No. 14. Chicago: Association of College and Reference Libraries, 1955.

Schlacter, Gail A., ed. *The Service Imperative for Libraries: Essays in Honor of Margaret E. Monroe*. Littleton, Colo.: Libraries Unlimited, 1982.

"Impact of Technology on Today's Reference Services"

Alberico, Ralph. "Workstations for Reference and Retrieval, Part One: The Scholar's Workstation." *Small Computers in Libraries*, March 1988, 4-10.

_____. "Workstations for Reference and Retrieval, Part Two." *Small Computers in Libraries*, April 1988, 4-9.

American Library Association. "Reference Services." In *ALA Yearbook of Library and Information Services, 1988*, 278-82. Chicago, 1988.

_____. *Report of the ALA Commission on Freedom and Equality of Access to Information*. Chicago: American Library Association, 1986.

Harta, Stephen, and Susan M. Jackson. "Optical Disk Systems in Libraries: Problems and Issues." *RQ* 27 (Summer 1988): 516-27.

Nielsen, Brian. "The Role of the Public Services Librarian: A New Revolution." In *Rethinking the Library in the Information Age,* vol. 2., 179-200. Washington, D.C.: U.S. Department of Education, 1989.

Roose, Tina. "Computerized Reference Tools of the Next Decade: Taking the Plunge with CD-ROM." *Library Journal* 113 (15 October 1988): 56-61.

Van Houweling, Douglas. "The Information Technology Environment of Higher Education." *The Campus of the Future*, 59-106. Dublin, Ohio: OCLC Online Computer Library Center, Inc., 1987.

"Changing Technology and Tomorrow's Reference Services"

Bezold, Clement, and Robert Olson. *The Information Millennium: Alternative Futures*. Washington, D.C.: Information Industry Association, 1986.

Brand, Stewart. *The Media Lab: Inventing the Future at MIT*. New York: Viking-Penguin, 1987.

Lancaster, F. W. "Future Librarianship: Preparing for an Unconventional Career." *Wilson Library Bulletin* 78 (May 1983): 747-53.

Wheeler, Harvey. *The Virtual Library: The Electronic Library Developing within the Traditional Library*. Los Angeles: University of Southern California, 1987.

Resource Sharing and Collection Development

"ILL: The Backbone of Materials Sharing"

Bell, Jo Ann, and Susan C. Speer. "Bibliographic Verification for Interlibrary Loan: Is It Necessary?" *College & Research Libraries* 49 (November 1988): 494-500.

Brunell, David H. *Linking Systems and Resource Sharing*. Network Planning Paper No. 15, pp. 35-40. Nationwide Networking. Washington, D.C.: Library of Congress, 1987.

Daehn, Ralph M. "Microcomputers and ILL: The Practical Aspects." *Canadian Library Journal* 45 (April 1988): 99-106.

Day, Janice, and Arden Matheson. "ACUILLA: A Microcomputer-Based Interlibrary Loans Management Package." *Microcomputers for Information Management* 5 (June 1988): 93-111.

Graber, Marla, A. James Bothmer, and Carol VerValin. "OCLC Interlibrary Loan: Group Access in Colorado." *Bulletin of the Medical Library Association* 76 (July 1988): 268-69.

Jackson, Mary E. "Facsimile Transmission: The Next Generation of Document Delivery." *Wilson Library Bulletin* 62 (May 1988): 37-43.

Lunau, Carrol D. "Canadian Advances in the Application of Electronic Mail and Interlibrary Loan Automation." *Interlending & Document Supply* 16 (April 1988): 58-64.

Miller, Constance R., and Patricia Tegler. "An Analysis of Interlibrary Loan and Commercial Document Supply Performance." *The Library Quarterly* 58 (October 1988): 352-66.

Preece, Barbara G., and Rose Hoshiko. "Rural Libraries and Automation: A Resource-Sharing Experience." *Public Libraries* 27 (Winter 1988): 188-90.

"Resource Sharing and ILL Fees in the Pacific Northwest." *PNLA Quarterly* 52, no. 3 (Spring 1988): 3-7.

Rutledge, John and Luke Swindler. "Evaluating Membership in a Resource-Sharing Program: The Center for Research Libraries." *College & Research Libraries* 49 (September 1988): 409-24.

Stranathan, Helen E., and Ralph W. Teller. "Computers and Interlibrary Loan: A Boon to the Rural Community." *Colorado Libraries* 14 (June 1988): 15-16.

Thayer, Candace W., and Kathryn Ray. "A Local Network for Sharing Resources and Technical Support: BACS/Philnet." *Bulletin of the Medical Library Association* 76 (October 1988): 343-45.

White, Herbert S. "Interlibrary Loan: An Old Idea in a New Setting." *Library Journal* 112, no. 12 (July 1987): 53-54.

"Collection Development and the Influence of Resource Sharing"

Ballard, Thomas H. "Dogma Clouds the Facts." *American Libraries* 16 (April 1985): 257-59.

Battin, Patricia. "Research Libraries in the Network Environment: The Case for Cooperation." *The Journal of Academic Librarianship* 6 (May 1980): 68-73.

"Cooperative Collection Management." Special Issue. *Illinois Libraries* 7 (January 1989).

Dougherty, Richard M. "A Conceptual Framework for Organized Resource Sharing and Shared Collection Development Programs." *The Journal of Academic Librarianship* 14 (November 1988): 287-91.

Hewitt, Joe A., and John S. Shipman. "Cooperative Collection Development among Research Libraries in the Age of Networking: Report of a

Survey of ARL Libraries." In *Advances in Library Automation and Networking*. Vol 1. Greenwich, Conn.: JAI Press, 1987.

Resource Sharing and Information Networks 2 (Spring/Summer 1985).

Sloan, Bernard G. "Resource Sharing among Academic Libraries: The LCS Experience." *The Journal of Academic Librarianship* 12 (March 1986): 26-29.

Serving Our Varied Clientele

"Slaying Dragons: Overcoming Obstacles to Excellence in Youth Services"

Cohen, Herb. *You Can Negotiate Anything*. Toronto: Bantam, 1982.

Kiersey, David, and Marilyn Bates. *Please Understand Me: Character and Temperament Types*. Del Mar, Calif.: Prometheas Nemesis, 1984.

Peters, Thomas J., and Robert H. Waterman. *In Search of Excellence: Lessons from America's Best Run Companies*. New York: Warner, 1984.

The Real-Life Library. Louisville, Ky.: Multi-Video Productions, 1987. Videotape.

Somerville, Mary R. "Facing the Shortage of Children's Librarians." *American Libraries* 18 (June 1987): 418-25.

"Free for All"

Daly, Macdonald, and Gordon Riddel. "Turning Back the Clock." *History Today*, October 1988, 6-9.

Govan, James F. "The Creeping Invisible Hand: Entrepreneurial Librarianship." *Library Journal* 113 (January 1988): 35-38.

Intner, Sheila A., and Jorge R. Schement. "The Ethic of Free Service." *Library Journal* 112 (October 1987): 50-52.

"Populism Offers a Progressive Alternative to Liberalism." *L. A. Weekly*, 31 July 1987.

Public Library Association. Goals, Guidelines, and Standards Committee. *The Public Library Mission Statement and Its Imperatives for Service*. Chicago: American Library Association, 1979.

Smith, Barbara. "A Strategic Approach to Online User Fees in Public Libraries." *Library Journal* 114 (February 1989): 33-36.

White, Herbert S. "What Price Salami? The Federal Process of Contracting Out Our Libraries." *Library Journal* 113 (January 1988): 58-59.

"Public Library Service to Special Groups"

American Library Association. Office for Library Outreach Services. *Libraries and Literacy: Closing the Education Gap*. Chicago: American Library Association, 1981.

American Library Association. Reference and Adult Services Division. Library Service to Aging Population Committee. *The Library's Responsibility to the Aging*. (RASD statement, revised June 1981.) *RQ* 21 (Fall 1981): 27.

Bradford, Gamaliel. *Damaged Souls*. Boston: Houghton Mifflin, 1922.

Dalton, Phyllis I. *Library Service to the Deaf and Hearing Impaired*. Phoenix: Oryx Press, 1985.

Lucas, Linda, ed. *Library Services to Developmentally Disabled Children and Adults*. Chicago: Association of Specialized and Cooperative Library Agencies, 1982. (ASCLA Occasional Paper, no. 1).

Needham, William L., and Gerald Jahoda. *Improving Library Service to Physically Disabled Persons: A Self-Evaluation Checklist*. Littleton, Colo.: Libraries Unlimited, 1983.

Turock, Betty J. *Serving the Older Adult: A Guide to Library Programs and Information Sources*. New York: Bowker, 1982.

"Serving the University Family: Truths among the Myths"

Feigenbaum, E. A. "The Library of the Future." Lecture given to mark the opening of Aston University's Computing Suite. United Kingdom: Aston University, 11 November 1986.

Gunning, Kathleen. "An Integrated Model of Library Information Services." The ACRL Third National Conference. *Proceedings*. Seattle, 4-7 April 1984, 93-95.

Hauser, John R., and Don Clausing. "The House of Quality." *Harvard Business Review* 66 (May-June 1988): 63-73.

Lunin, Lois, ed. "Perspective on . . . Integrated Academic Information Management Systems (IAIMS)." *Journal of the American Society for Information Science* 39 (March 1988): 102-45

Martell, Charles. "A House Divided: Public Services Realities in the 1980's." The ACRL Third National Conference. *Proceedings*. Seattle, 4-7 April 1984, 85-88.

Monroe, Margaret E. *Library Adult Education: The Biography of an Idea*. New York: Scarecrow Press, 1963.

Swanson, Patricia K. "Traditional Models: Myths and Realities." The ACRL Third National Conference. *Proceedings*. Seattle, 4-7 April 1984, 89-92.

Weiskel, Timothy C. "The Electronic Library." *Change* 21 (November/December 1988): 38-47.

Impact of a New Major Facility on Library Services

"Samuel Lazerow Memorial Lecture: Breaking Ground in Chicago – Planning the Harold Washington Library Center"

Adams, S., and J. Natale. "Building Illinois' Libraries: Public Library Construction." *Illinois Libraries* 69 (January 1987): 29-33.

Ellsworth, R. E. *Academic Library Buildings: A Guide to Architectural Issues and Solutions*. Boulder, Colo.: Colorado Associated University Press, 1973.

Hall, Richard B., ed. *Financing and Promotion of Public Library Facilities: Facilities Funding Finesse*. Chicago: American Library Association, 1982.

Holt, R. M. *Handbook for Planning Public Library Buildings*. Madison, Wis.: Wisconsin Department of Public Instruction, Division of Library Services, 1978.

Metcalf, Keyes D., Philip D. Leighton, and David C. Weber. *Planning Academic and Research Library Buildings*. Rev. ed. Chicago: American Library Association, 1986.

Rohlf, Robert H. "Library Design: What Not to Do – Successful Library Building Programs Avoid These Common Pitfalls." *American Libraries* 17 (February 1986): 100, 102-4.

Impact of Technology on Staffing

"Implications of Technology on Staffing"

Applegate, Lina, James I. Cash, Jr., and D. Quinn Mills. "Information Technology and Tomorrow's Manager." *Harvard Business Review* 66 (November-December 1988): 128-36.

Horney, Karen L. "Fifteen Years of Automation: Evolution of Technical Service Staffing." *Library Resources and Technical Services* 31 (January-March 1987): 69-76.

Kuhlman, Torsten M. "Adapting to Technical Change in the Workplace." *Personnel* 65 (August 1988): 67-70.

Sankar, V. "Organizational Culture and New Technologies." *Journal of Systems Management* 39 (April 1988): 10-17.

Zuboff, Shoshana. *In the Age of the Smart Machine: The Future of Work and Power*. New York: Basic Books, 1988.

"Information Specialist: Modern-Day Librarian or New Professional?"

Bearman, Toni Carbo. "The Changing Role of the Information Professional." *Library Trends* 32 (Winter 1984): 255-60.

Caputo, Janette S. *The Assertive Librarian*. Phoenix: Oryx Press, 1984.

DeWeese, L. Carroll. "Status Concerns and Library Professionalism." *College and Research Libraries* 33 (January 1982): 31. Quoted in Lester Asheim, "Librarians as Professionals," *Library Trends* 27 (Winter 1979): 225-58.

Galvin, Thomas J. "The Significance of Information Science for the Theory and Practice of Librarianship." *Libri* 34 (1984): 81-87.

Griffiths, José-Marie. "Competency Requirements for Library and Information Science Professionals." In *Professional Competencies – Technology and Librarian*, edited by Linda C. Smith, 5-12. Urbana-Champaign, Ill.: University of Illinois Graduate School of Library and Information Science, 1985.

Intner, Sheila S., and Jane Anne Hannigan. *The Library Microcomputer Environment: Management Issues*. Phoenix: Oryx Press, 1988.

King, Donald W., et al. "A National Profile of Information Professionals." *Bulletin of the American Society for Information Science* 6 (August 1980): 18-22.

Lunin, Lois F. "The Work of Information Specialists." In *Careers in Information*, edited by Jane F. Spivack, 25-50. White Plains, N.Y.: Knowledge Industry Publications, 1982.

Meadow, A. J., ed. *The Origins of Information Science*. London: Taylor Graham and Contributors, 1987.

Moore, Nick. *The Emerging Markets for Librarians and Information Workers*. London: The British Library Board, 1987.

Nitecki, Danuta A. "Competencies Required of Public Services Librarians to Use New Technologies." In *Professional Competencies – Technology and Librarian*, edited by Linda C. Smith, 43-57. Urbana-Champaign, Ill.: University of Illinois Graduate School of Library and Information Science, 1985.

Oboler, Eli M. *To Free the Mind: Libraries, Technology and Intellectual Freedom*. Littleton, Colo.: Libraries Unlimited, 1983.

Sieburth, Janice F. *Online Search Services in the Academic Library – Planning, Management and Operation*. Chicago: American Library Association, 1988.

_____. "Alternative Careers for Library-Information Workers." *ASLIB Proceedings* 36 (June 1984): 277-286.

Slater, Margaret. *Careers Guidance and Library/Information Work*. London: The British Library Board, 1986.

Spivack, Jane. *Careers in Information*. White Plains, N.Y.: Knowledge Industry Publications, 1982.

Svenonius, Elaine, and Rutherford Witthus. "Information Science as a Profession." In *Annual Review of Information Science and Technology*. White Plains, New York: Knowledge Industry Publications, 1981.

Sweeney, Richard T. "The Public Librarian of the Last Years of the Twentieth Century." In *Professional Competencies – Technology and Librarian*, edited by Linda C. Smith, 58-69. Urbana-Champaign, Ill.: University of Illinois Graduate School of Library and Information Science, 1985.

U.S. Department of Commerce. *Standard Occupation Classification Manual* and *Dictionary of Occupational Titles (DOT)*. 4th ed. Washington, D.C.: Government Printing Office, 1980.